A Fowey Jig-Saw

A Fowey Jig-Saw

*The History of the
Royal Fowey Yacht Club*

Compiled by Joan Coombs

R.F.Y.C. BOOKS

Published by R.F.Y.C. Books,
Whitford Yard, Fowey PL23 1BH

First published 2000

© Joan Coombs

ISBN 0 9539622 0 2

Typeset and printed in Great Britain by
Penwell Limited, Callington, Cornwall

Contents

H.R.H. The Prince Philip, Duke of Edinburgh, K.G., K.T., O.M., G.B.E.,
Patron of the Royal Fowey Yacht Club.

Of all the many yacht clubs in the South West, the Royal Fowey must be one of the best known with its splendidly situated Club House at the edge of the river. It is certainly one of the oldest and, after 120 years since its precursor, the Fowey Club, was founded, it is high time for its history and development to be traced and a record made of its contribution to yachting in the West Country. Like all good yacht clubs, it has also had a fair share of remarkable characters as members to enliven its history.

I was fortunate enough to be able to visit the Club and to sail my Dragon 'Bluebottle' at Fowey while General Sir Frederick Browning ('Boy' or 'Tommy' depending on the context) was both Commodore of the Club and Comptroller of our Household at Clarence House. He was an enthusiastic yachtsman and the first time I visited Cowes Regatta in 1949 I stayed with him in his converted MFV 'Fanny Rosa'.

Even though I have seldom had the opportunity to visit the Club, I was delighted to be invited to be Patron in 1953 and I have taken an interest in it ever since. I am sure that present and future members of the Club will appreciate this record of a much-loved institution.

Philip

Acknowledgements

This story of Fowey and the Royal Fowey Yacht Club has been a long time in preparation. Much of what has been included has been published elsewhere and I am indebted to authors or their executors for permission to reproduce the pieces of the jigsaw puzzle which together make the picture of the club in its setting.

It is fortunate that Sir Arthur Quiller-Couch wrote so much about the harbour that he loved so well and I am grateful to Guy Symondson for permission to quote from his works.

I am greatly indebted to many people from whom I have received much help with both the text, with photographs and with anecdotes. I hope that I have listed them all.

First of all I thank HRH Prince Philip, our Patron, for his gracious foreword and permission to reproduce his photograph.

I am grateful to Mrs Muriel Brittain of Jesus College, Cambridge, for permission to quote from her husband, F Brittain's book entitled 'Q ~ A Biographical Study of Arthur Quiller-Couch'.

Mr James C Slater kindly gave permission to quote from 'Grey Ghosts ~ Voices'.

I thank the President and Fellows of Trinity College, Oxford, for permission to publish photographs of Bevil Quiller-Couch and also I thank Dr Matthew Steggle, Mrs Claire Hopkins and Mr Bryan Ward-Perkins of the Trinity College Archive, Oxford for their personal help.

I thank the Western Morning News for permission to quote from articles held at The Reference Library in Plymouth and also Cornwall Record Office for help received there.

It was a great pleasure to view the photograph albums of the late Tony Parkin, great nephew of Herbert Dampier Phelps who was Honorary Secretary in the early days of the Club. Some of the pictures have been included.

I have received a lot of help with the photographs. I am grateful to the Royal Institution of Cornwall for the use of early photographs of Fowey and also the National Maritime Museum, London for permission to reproduce photographs from their collections, also to the Tatler magazine for permission to reproduce pages from their September 14th, 1946 edition.

Jim Matthews and Billie Graeme previously of Noah's Ark, Fowey have lent photographs as have Tessa and Gerry Williams.

I am grateful to Marcus Lewis and Sue Rodwell for use of photographs and also to Mrs Mavis Johns who kindly lent me the photograph of Prince Philip, Princess Elizabeth and Commodore Browning on "Fanny Rosa" and to Mr David Turpin for the photograph of "Jigsaw".

I am indebted to Flavia, Lady Leng for the photograph of her father, General Sir Frederick A.M. Browning.

The line drawings are reproduced with the kind permission of Yachting Monthly Magazine where these sketches first appeared in 1911.

My thanks go to Duncan R. Winning, Honorary President of the Scottish Canoe Association for his help with Canoe History.

I am grateful to the late David Treffry for his encouragement and permission to photograph family portraits at Place.

I am grateful to Twinkle Treffry for the photographs that she has taken that are included in the book.

Mrs Elizabeth Chatwin has kindly permitted me to quote from her husband's essay "Your father's eyes are blue again" for which I am grateful.

Alison Prince has given permission for me to quote from her book "Kenneth Grahame – An innocent in the wild" and to use two pictures from her book for which I am grateful.

Every effort has been made to acknowledge sources and photographs. If any inclusion has not received correct attribution I apologise in advance.

I am indebted to many others for help and encouragement, they include the Rev. David Maddock, The Royal Western Yacht Club of England, Mr Harold Eardley, Toby West of Falmouth and Commodore Denis Simpson for proof-reading.

I am grateful for typing help I have received from Sarah Cheffins, Barbara Philp and Judy Martin. My thanks for computer help go to John Stewart of Fowey and Andrew Coombs.

Lastly I pay tribute to the contribution that my husband has made supporting and encouraging me and for his patience.

Although this is the story of a yacht club I hope it will appeal to general readers. The study of the life and times of the club has been fascinating for me. I hope that this glimpse of changing times in the last one hundred years will be enjoyable to others also.

Introduction

Fowey Harbour is one of the most beautiful on the South Coast of Cornwall. Fowey town has grown very little from that which clustered around the Town Quay and the Church of St Fimbarrus on the west bank of the estuary in earlier times.

Across the water is Polruan clinging to the east banks which climb from the waters edge.

The streets of Fowey and Polruan are narrow and awkward for modern traffic.

The main highway of Fowey is the river itself always busy with traffic whether it be the ocean going cargo boats carrying china clay from the jetties up river beyond the town, pleasure craft of all descriptions, the tugs, the dredger, the ferries or the cruise liners visiting in Summer.

For many of those who come upon it first from the open seas into the sheltered haven between the headlands of St Catherine's and St Saviour's it is love at first sight.

For many visiting yacht people the Royal Fowey Yacht Club is a pleasant and friendly place. Set at the waters edge with a sunny terrace, a warm welcome and refreshments at hand it seems to have always been there, a relic of a previous bygone life style. It seems little changed from the past and yet is has had to adapt to modern ways and still preserve its charm.

It has not always been there. This is the story of how it came to be from the earliest days as a gentleman's club in different premises nearer the Town Quay.

Preparing a short history of it's evolution to celebrate the 100 years since the establishment of the present building was the inspiration of this more detailed account. There have been other centenaries, one in 1980 to celebrate the beginning of the Fowey Gentleman's Club and another in 1984 to celebrate the beginning of the Yacht Club in 1894.

A previous history of the club by Walter Grahame and an earlier decision by Donald Carter to research the archives were also inspiration. Donald Carter's reference notes still interleave the records. Gradually the ghosts of the past began to speak and the past came alive for me.

I have developed a deep affection for my initial love affair with Fowey. Readers are bound to notice my profound admiration and fondness for the hero of the story Q. I hope they share it.

The Royal Fowey Yacht Club is a remarkable institution, valuable for the amenity and friendship which it offers just as it did over 100 years ago.

Panoramic view of Fowey Harbour, 1893, with Fowey to the right of the picture facing Polruan across the water.

Early Days

Fowey is an ancient Cornish seaport set on the steep west bank of the River Fowey. Facing the town across the wide harbour is the old shipbuilding village of Polruan. The estuary, a sunken valley, is not only wide but deep and provides deep water passage for a variety of commercial shops which sail past the town to the docks upriver.

The harbour is a haven for boats of all kinds. It is guarded from the open sea by twin headlands - St Catherine's to the west and St Saviour's on the Polruan side. In earlier times chapels stood on these promontories probably providing guiding lights for shipping.

Five miles upstream is the town of Lostwithiel which was once the capital of Cornwall. It was also a centre where Cornish tin was assayed and marked with an official stamp prior to export. Tin was extracted all over Cornwall by a process of panning. Gradually the washings and sediment from this industry silted up the river and the waterway to Lostwithiel became un-navigable to all but vessels of shallow draught. Consequently, Fowey became the principal port and steadily grew in prosperity.

Trading was not confined to tin although this was the main export. There were many other commodities moved to and from the port. These included horse hides, cheeses, bacon hogs, butter and feathers together with cloth, beds and armour too.

During the thirteen and fourteenth centuries Fowey was well known for its prosperity and 'fearsome sailors.' In 1347 King Edward III commandeered 47 vessels and 770 men from the port of Fowey to join the English fleet at the siege of Calais. These sailors became known as the Fowey Gallants.

Not only were Fowey ships employed in the defence of the realm they were also commissioned to transport pilgrims. This was a popular phenomenon in the Middle Ages involving Christian travel to holy places. The destination from Fowey was the shrine of St James of Compostella in Spain.

By the 14th Century piracy was rife on the seas. This was known as privateering. It was licensed by the state and vessels were encouraged to capture vessels of other nationalities for profit. Fowey benefited greatly from this activity. Probably as an act of reprisal, a French expedition set out to harass English shipping and to raid ports on the South Coast. Fowey was attacked in 1457 when the mansion called Place was successfully defended by Elizabeth Treffry but there was much burning and destruction in the town.

Blockhouses were erected on the east and west banks of the river probably as a defence against such attacks. A chain was stretched between the two blockhouses across the harbour to prevent unwelcome ships entering.

Two notable families in Fowey in Elizabethan times were the Treffrys of Place and the Rashleighs. Philip Rashleigh was a merchant and ship owner. The

A steam tug tows a schooner out of the harbour. Prior to 1891.

Rashleigh town house is now the Ship Inn in Fowey. Successful in enterprise, Jonathon Rashleigh acquired a great deal of property in and around the town and built himself a mansion at Menabilly.

During the early 19th Century the harbour continued to be crowded with shipping: fighting ships, fishing boats and privateers. Trade was buoyant. Vessels were built both in boatyards in Fowey, Polruan and Bodinnick and also on foreshores in the estuary. All the ancillary trades supplying these ships were fully occupied.

The fishing industry was active in home waters and abroad. Pilchards were fished locally in great abundance, salted and stored. They were known as fumadoes and were a popular export to Catholic Mediterranean countries. The fishing grounds of Newfoundland were a rich source of cod for the Fowey fishermen. Salt curing took place in Fowey and the product was distributed both in England and Wales as well as abroad.

Slowly this wave of prosperity abated and by the middle of the 19th Century the fortunes of Fowey were at a low ebb. The advent of steam power for shipping meant that small sailing vessels were no longer in demand. Ocean-going ships were built in the great shipyards of Liverpool and the Clyde. Shipbuilding and all the ancillary trades around Fowey harbour fell into decline. The fishing industry faltered as well as the pilchard shoals began to desert the fishing grounds. In the early year's of the 19th Century seasons of abundant fish alternated with great scarcity. Heavy import duties imposed in Italy, the development of new curing methods and the withdrawal of the government bounty heralded the end of the fishing trade. There was unemployment and hardship in the harbour communities. Only those whose livelihood did not depend entirely on ships and fishing survived unscathed.

Fowey

17

SOUVENIRS.

Drawn by Arthur Briscoe.

Some Ports and their Characteristic Craft.

18

The Revival of Fowey

William Rashleigh did not want to live at Menabilly. He chose the site of an 18th Century gun battery and in 1862 the large granite villa, called Point Neptune, was completed at Readymoney Cove. On October 31 the drive to Point Neptune now known as St Catherine's Parade was dedicated to public use. There were considerable ceremonials but it is the remarks made by Mr Rashleigh to his friend, Reverend E J Treffry, regarding the conditions in Fowey that are of special interest.

Here is the account of the event in the Cornwall Gazette:

"The Fowey Artillery Volunteers attended with their band and by 2.00 o'clock a large number of persons of all classes, ranks and ages had congregated at the northern end of the new road. Mr Rashleigh was seated in an open phaeton. At the entrance to the new road was erected a handsome arch bearing the mottoes: "Welcome" and "Ships, Colonies, Commerce" wrought in flowers and surmounted by a banner with the motto "God bless our Queen Victoria."

Before entering the gateway Mr Rashleigh requested the crowd to join him in

Point Neptune, the granite villa built in 1862 at Readymoney Cove. William Rashleigh preferred this house to the mansion at Menabilly.

19

An early view of the harbour viewed from Polruan prior to 1898. The site of the R.Y.F.C. is still as a boat yard. New houses are in the process of erection along the Esplanade.

An enlarged version of the previous picture. Two sheds and stored timber stand in Whitfords boat yard. The premises of the Fowey Club are in the large house to the right of the pictute.

three hearty cheers for "Her Most Gracious Majesty, Queen Victoria - Queen of Great Britain, Empress of India and mistress of the seas." Cheers were given most heartily and the band of the Fowey Artillery Volunteers played God Save the Queen. The procession then formed and the crowd followed the band down the new road. At Point Neptune there was another triumphal arch bearing floral mottoes "Prosperity to the Port of Fowey" and "Welcome"; these being surmounted by the motto "God save our Queen Victoria."

Unfortunately there was close and heavy rain. From his carriage Mr Rashleigh addressed the assemblage around him. "Having presented to you this pathway I claim the right to christen it the St Catherine's Parade. I have long wished for the prosperity of Fowey, but I see in it a great lack of that go ahead spirit. I must say there is in Fowey greater inaction than I ever saw in any other port. You must rouse yourselves and do something for the place. If it is to be a Railway Terminus it will not do to have a Railway Terminus among a parcel of tumble-down buildings. Just look at the landing place. I ask, is that landing place not a disgrace to a port having such a name as yours has? We must try to put our shoulders to the wheel. A public company brings you a railroad, a private individual gives you a pathway, but I want to see a little more energy and esprit de corps among Fowey people.

You have the best anchorage that I know anywhere; you have a most lovely river. I have no doubt that with spirit and energy on your part you may have villas built there and their occupants spending money among you. I should certainly like to see villas similar to my own close at hand here. But all that would not do without a first class hotel.

View of Fowey from Pont River, 1889. Shipping is moored in the harbour. A ship's hull is under construction in Whitford's Yard.

You want such a house with suitable rooms where public spirited men may meet and transact business and with proper commercial rooms"

The passion of this delivery and his avowed wish for the greater prosperity of Fowey is perhaps related to feelings of regret that Joseph Thomas Austin Treffry did not do more for the town, for he said:

"I have long wished that my late venerable friend, the greatest employer in this county, instead of taking away the trade of Fowey, had brought his talents, his capital and his energy to bear on this port; for I believe that in that case Fowey would have stood next to the port of Falmouth. I say that without the slightest disrespect to the gentleman who now so well represents and manages the Treffry property."

The gentleman in question was his luncheon guest, the Reverend E J Treffry. The newspaper account continues:

"A large number of invited guests then took lunch at Point Neptune, where there was a most bounteous and elegant display of substantial and tempting refection and excellent wines laid out in the large dining hall, commanding an interesting view of the entrance to Fowey Harbour.

After a succession of loyal and other toasts the Reverend E J Treffry gave cordial thanks to Mr Rashleigh."

Now the Reverend E J Treffry had inherited most of the estate of Joseph Thomas Austin Treffry. He was born Edward John Wilcocks and was the son of a cousin of Joseph Austin. His mother was Jane Treffry Dormer Wilcocks. He was married and worked as a vicar at St Mary's, Isles of Scilly, and later was headmaster of Berkhamsted School.

In order to inherit the estate he was required to take the name Treffry. So he became Reverend Edward John Treffry and inherited Place in 1850. He became vicar of Fowey in 1863 and remained so until 1867 when he resigned. His son-in-law, the Reverend Hanfield Noel Purcell then became the vicar of Fowey, and was to remain so for 54 years.

The Reverend Edward John Treffry's response to Mr Rashleigh was reported: "With reference to some observances which Mr Rashleigh has made, I regret even more than he does, the tumble-down state of many of the houses in Fowey. We will repair these tumble-down houses as soon as we can see our way clear to have tenants to occupy them. Now we have a railroad coming close to our doors Fowey must become the shipping port for the China Clay and China Stone of the neighbourhood and Fowey must become a prosperous place."

What else could he say? He was a good man. He had been fortunate to inherit the estate and was eager to improve the fortunes of Fowey. The new Squire did invest in the future of the port: between 1854 and 1876 he had shares in about 40 Fowey vessels. He was the owner of the first steam tug and had revolutionised port shipping.

The Railway

During this time there was in increase in the export of china clay and the jetties at Carne, on the west bank of the river above the town, were developed. The Cornwall Mineral Railway linking Lostwithiel and Fowey by broad gauge was established in the 1860's so that the china clay could be brought down from the clay pits by truck and loaded onto the ships at Carne.

The development of the china clay trade brought greater prosperity to the town. Ship building revived and until the 1880's the shipyards in Fowey and Polruan were busy. All the ancillary traders housed in the town were busy too; sailmakers, blockmakers, chandlers and rope manufacturers all provided employment leading to a revival of the community.

Many of the old decayed cottages made of cob were demolished to be replaced by modern houses of brick or granite with better amenities.

Attempts were made to improve the water supply to the town. Previously people had to rely on fetching water from the town cock which often dribbled dry.

In 1870 the Cornwall Gazette reported criticism of the inadequate water supply to the town of Fowey and stated that more than half the properties had no drainage. The streets were disgustingly dirty and ill-paved and the street cleaner, known as the scavenger, was no longer able to work through advanced age. By 1875 there were plans to improve things. An inspection by the St Austell Board of Guardians reported that in Lostwithiel Street there was no kind of drain whatever. Refuse and other offensive matter from the houses was deposited in the street. It was recommended that a main sewer be laid and that the drains should be flushed out in the dry summer months with seawater. Nearly all the houses were without closet accommodation but the owners of the properties agreed to proceed with improvements once the main sewer was laid.

By October 1875 a contractor was employed to burrow to the extent of 20 feet under the level of Trafalgar Square. The works were under the immediate superintendence of Mr C Crapp!

In 1887 although a small reservoir had been built at the head of the sewer it did not effectively flush the drains, especially in dry weather. There was no proper refuse collection and there was a disagreeable refuse dump near the ashpit on the Town Quay. This was condemned by the Harbour Commissioners who sent the town crier around the town announcing that anyone throwing rubbish into the harbour would be prosecuted!

Panoramic view across the River Fowey towards Caffa Mill Pier. A barque is moored at the loading pier. On the railway are wagons loaded with china clay. In the middle distance is the railway station. Two topsl. schooners are moored in the Pill (now a car park).

Improvement in Fowey

However, conditions gradually improved so that by 1878 a traveller from London wrote in the Western Daily Mercury: "Whenever I visit Fowey I indulge in the hope of one day building a nest here. Apart from its improved sanitary condition and the most civil and obliging characteristics of its inhabitants." The journalist added: "It is contemplated, we understand, to invite the well reputed firm of Julian and Sons of Truro to add to the fine buildings they are now erecting here for educational purposes, several well situated villas on elevations overlooking the harbour and the entrance from the English Channel, if land can be obtained on reasonable terms. Why should not the ancient and picturesque port of Fowey participate in the advantages of that great influx of holiday visitors who now crowd from far off places for health and repose into the seashore haunts."

Then in 1883 the broad gauge mineral line between Lostwithiel and Fowey was reconstructed for passenger traffic. It was possible to travel from Paddington station in London to Fowey in as little as six hours and the Great Western Railway promoted the idea of the Cornish Riviera as a rival holiday spot to the South of France.

The Victorian era produced many changes in English life as the economy changed. The industrial revolution brought wealth to more people than ever before. Power and influence passed from the aristocracy to the middle classes.

Tourism begins

Summer holidays and tourism became popular and was made possible by the advent of the steam train as affordable public transport. People travelled to the South West as never before, and Fowey was a favourite destination.

The Fowey Hotel was established in 1882 and was such a success from the beginning that it was necessary to add an extension. The addition was completed in 1891 and added about 20 new bedrooms, a fine new dining room, billiard room and smoke room. This extension doubled the accommodation of the original building erected ten years before.

Mr Isbell, a successful Fowey builder, was the contractor. To celebrate the opening "the Fowey Hotel was for the first time lighted up by electricity, being a great improvement on the old gas jets."

The Cornwall Gazette continues:

"It is hoped that Fowey will soon be lighted by the electric light as the price of gas is very high, and the quality not of the best."

Yachting

Towards the end of the 19th Century more and more successful businessmen took up yachting. Originally it was only those of great wealth who displayed their fortunes to the world, racing their giant yachts both in America and in Britain. This racing scene was closely linked with fashionable society and therefore of great interest to the general public.

The birthplace of yachting in Britain was the Thames, but by the 1850's congestion by commercial shipping made racing difficult.

The sport then moved to the south coast and to Cowes in particular. The development of the railway system made it possible for would-be sailors and their families to travel to the seaside resorts for the summer.

Cowes Week marked the beginning to the racing season. Yachting resorts such as Plymouth, Fowey and Falmouth would co-ordinate their regattas and Channel races linked one regatta with another.

As well as providing sport for the boat owners, yachting brought employment for many fishermen and boatmen living in the small towns along the coast.

In 1899 members of the Royal Yacht Squadron at Cowes owned about 150 yachts which gave employment to over 2,000 seamen.

Boat building and boat repair yards were once again busy, as were sailmakers and all the businesses supplying the sport. Similar development took place in Fowey when yachting came to the port and the first Fowey Yacht Club was established.

The Fowey Club

Trade and living conditions gradually improved during the next ten years or so in Fowey. As William Rashleigh had predicted in 1862 prosperity brought businessmen to the town. Comfortable villas were built at the waters edge to house them and as he suggested they needed a first class place where they could rest and transact business, a gentlemans club.

Gentlemen's clubs were popular throughout the country. They provided an atmosphere of seclusion, comfort and service in almost every town in the empire. Clubs were exclusive common rooms for elected subscribers only. Only the 'great and the good' and those who could afford it were admitted. Those in 'trade' and women were excluded.

The Fowey Club was founded around 1880 in order to "facilitate the association of gentlemen who wish to enjoy the social advantages of a club without political bias."

Dolphin Row numbers 1 and 2, the site of the Gentleman's Club in Fowey which later became the Yacht Club.

Charles Ebeneezer Treffry of Place.
A popular man in Fowey and known
as 'The Squire'. He was Chairman of
the Fowey Club.

Place mansion at Fowey. The home of generations of the Treffry family.

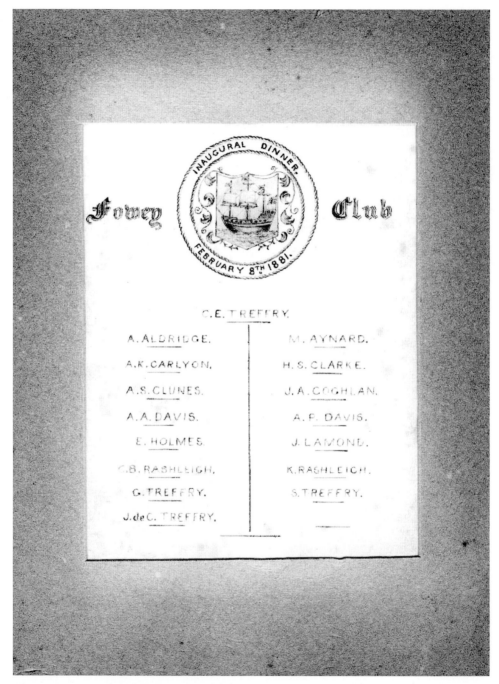

The seating arrangement on the menu of the inaugural dinner of the Fowey Club, February 8 1851. The menu is reproduced on the back cover.

Q became Hon. Sec. of the Fowey Club in 1893 at the age of 29. He continued as Hon. Secretary of the Fowey Yacht Club until 1897.

An inaugural dinner of the Fowey Club was held on February 8th 1881 and fifteen members attended. Mr Charles Ebeneezer Treffry presided over the dinner. He was 39 years of age. His father the Rev. Edward John (Wilcocks) Treffry had died the year before. Although he had inherited Place from his father he had not moved in and was still living with his family in Bagatelle House nearby. Three of his younger brothers who lived in Fowey also attended the dinner. The two Dr Davis' present were father and son, both medical practitioners in the town. Also present were Emra Holmes, a customs collector living in Bellevue House and Alex Clunes, an architect and civil engineer who lived with his young wife and two small children in Dolphin Row.

The premises of the Fowey Club were at No 2 Dolphin Terrace in Trafalgar Square. It is an elegant frontage, only a little changed today and a convenient venue for the " man-about- Fowey." The south side of the building overlooked the harbour and a wooden landing stage and steps gave the members access to the water.

It was there that the club flourished for the best part of eight years.

The Fowey Club wound up after nine years but most of the members promptly joined the reformed Fowey Club in February 1890 which continued in the same premises.

A very detailed picture of the club is given by the inventory prepared in September 1889.

The front door led into an entrance hall furnished with an umbrella stand and a barometer on the wall. 10 yards of linoleum and one large coconut fibre mat covered the floor, and 18 yards of stair canvas covered the stairs to the upper floors. There was a carpeted library with chairs, chess table and draughtboards and a telescope at the window. The smoking room floor was covered with 8 yards of linoleum and 20 yards of Kidderminster carpet. There was a large mahogany table, with 11 armchairs and a gentleman's easy chair, a writing table and mahogany card table, and 4 metal ashtrays. This room was used for card games. It contained 2 whist markers and it was also used for letter writing for there were inkstands and letter racks too. The view over the harbour was scanned through another telescope and a pair of binoculars. There were 4 spitboxes or spittoons also!

The dining room was furnished with 2 large tables, 10 chairs and 4 armchairs. The floor was covered with floor canvas and 12 yards of Kidderminster carpet, and there was a fireplace with fender and fire irons. The walls were decorated with charts of the Cornish coast and one of Fowey Harbour, and once again there were spitboxes or spittoons, 3 in all.

In the lavatory there was also a double wash stand with toilet set, hat-brush, 2 hairbrushes, a looking glass, and coconut matting on the floor. There was also a tin letterbox and 1 'stone filter.' The significance of the latter item is a mystery.

An idea of the catering facilities comes from the kitchen inventory that included 18 wineglasses, 8 soda water glasses, 12 cut-glass tumblers, 3 brandy bottles and 3 cruets. Also trays, pewter pots, cutlery, 12 dinner napkins and white table cloths, 3 barrel stands and a beer tap, and 1 fish kettle. The Flagstaff and flag were kept in the kitchen and outside was a small wooden landing stage and steps, which were the property of the club. The total value was £35 3s 6d

Mrs Peard lived on the premises and was housekeeper. On September 27, 1892 the Honorary Secretary spoke to her about her grandchildren (presumably they had been too noisy). In 1894 her Christmas box was £5 in recognition of her services to the club. When she died on November 15,1895 she had been caretaker of the club for seven years.

Cynthia - first in Channel Race from Falmouth

The new Fowey Club 1890

The first general meeting of the newly formed Fowey Club took place on February 15, 1890.

Mr Edward Atkinson was in the chair and the meeting was attended by:
Mr Murray Rogers
Mr George Treffry (Squire's younger brother)
Mr F Allchin
Mr H S Cameron
Mr W Gundry
Mr W T Graham
Mr Arthur Davis
Mr Arthur H Hern

Although it is not clear whether he was present. It was proposed at this meeting that Charles Ebeneezer Treffry be asked to become president of the club. He was a popular man known to all as "the squire". Like many of the members he was a keen sailor.

It was resolved that the annual subscription should be two guineas for all members living within three miles of Fowey and one guinea for all members outside that area, payable on election and afterwards on October 1. The rules were to be sent to every member by registered post.

Mr A T Q Couch was unanimously elected a member of the club on February 15,1890. He was 26. His wife, Louisa, lived with her mother, Ann Hicks, in Fowey. Arthur Quiller Couch (there was no hyphen then) worked in London as a journalist.

By October 3, 1890 the committee was glad to be able to inform the members present that the affairs of the club were in a satisfactory state and that they intended to carry on the club for another year.

One feature of club life was the list of periodicals delivered. These seem to have been paid for by various individuals, each paying for the journal of their choice. The fact that they were available at the club ensured that there was always a variety of reading matter, comment and news.

It is interesting that although the Licensed Victuallers Gazette and Referee was recommended, not enough members were interested. However they did elect to take the Western Morning News, Western Daily Mercury, Daily Telegraph, Standard, Punch, Truth, Pall Mall Budget, Graphic, Field, Sporting Times, Globe on Saturday for Sunday. At the end of the year old journals were auctioned.

The club committee met on three occasions in 1891. In 1892 they met five times. These meetings mainly involved the vetting and election of new members. It was in 1892 that the vicar of St Fimbarrus Church was elected. He was the Reverend Hanfield Noel Purcell, who had married Squire Charles Treffry's elder sister Ann Ellen.

At the AGM on December 6, 1892 the club capital was increased by £10. Wealthy bachelor Edward Atkinson contributed £5 but so did the 29-year-old Arthur Quiller Couch who could have had little money to spare. His contribution signified his great commitment to the club.

On January 18, 1893 Arthur Quiller Couch was elected Honorary Secretary. From then on the minutes are in his handwriting which was meticulous, tiny and neat with no errors. Arthur Quiller Couch was known as Q to most of his friends and it was also his pen name. It was at about this time that he adopted the hyphen between Quiller and Couch.

The premises in Dolphin Terrace were in need of redecoration. It was agreed that the present clubhouse was unsatisfactory and by August 19, 1893 the question of a change of premises was discussed. It was suggested that a house on the Esplanade ~ 'Abergarwydd' ~ might be suitable. However the trustees of the late owner declined the proposal. A decision to approach the Harbour Commissioners for a site on the Town Quay also resulted in disappointment.

The committee met on five occasions in 1893. The membership continued to grow and it was decided to have house dinners every two months or so. The first was held at the Fowey Hotel. This was a fashionable venue and had become a Mecca for genteel holidaymakers in the ten years since its establishment.

Thirteen club members attended that first dinner and seventeen the next. Ladies were not present, of course, but the evenings included not only good food and wine but music too. The committee arranged to have the use of a piano, and Dr Boger and Mr Allchin, both club members, were well known for their vocal skills. In an earlier account in the Western Morning News they appeared at a concert in Polruan, when they sang from Offenbach's operetta 'The Two Blind Beggars'. At another concert in the Sunday School in Polruan in 1897: "Mr Allchin sang 'Giles on Politics' in character in his usual inimitable manner, and he most good naturedly responded to a vociferous encore." Mr Allchin had been Honorary Secretary of the club but had resigned because he lived so far away. He lived at Tredudwell, a house in countryside on the Polruan side of the river, and although his attendance required an overland journey and the water crossing, he remained a frequent attender of the club.

At the AGM in November 1893 the question of providing new premises for the club was again discussed at length. It was agreed that the present clubhouse at No2 Dolphin Square was undesirable in many respects. The lavatory passage and staircase urgently required improvement and redecoration.

The Fowey Club becomes The Fowey Yacht Club

In April 1894 it was decided that the club should in future be known as the Fowey Yacht Club.

A club badge was designed ~ a red burgee bearing a black shield with fifteen gold bezants.

In May officers were elected:

Mr Charles Ebeneezer Treffry was made Commodore

Mr Murray Rogers ~ Vice Commodore

Mr Edward Atkinson ~ Rear Commodore

But by the end of the month Mr Treffry had decided against being Commodore and at a meeting in June 1894 Mr Edward Atkinson was elected to the post. Mr Murray Rogers remained Vice Commodore and Arthur Quiller-Couch continued to serve as Honorary Secretary. Competitive boating was popular in Fowey. The town had a well established one day regatta held each August and known as Fowey Royal Regatta. By 1838 it was well established. The town was decorated with arches and evergreens in the streets and boats in the harbour were decked with flags. Sailing and rowing races in the harbour were followed by prize giving at The Ship Inn after a carnival procession led by the town band. The day ended with a grand display of fireworks from the Town Quay.

Both Edward Atkinson and Arthur Quiller-Couch were closely involved with the Town Regatta and naturally wished for the newly formed Yacht Club to play a part.

It was proposed that the club should offer prizes to be competed for in the forthcoming regatta of 1894, under RYA rules. The first prize was to be pieces of plate (silver tea and coffee service) to the value of £22. The second prize was to be to the value of ten guineas and the third prize three guineas. The money for the prizes was raised by subscription.

These were big prizes. The average skilled man's weekly wage at the time was around 25 shillings a week. Five cutters entered for the race during the 1894 August Regatta in Fowey. The race was won by J Lusky Coad in Shulah. He was a member of the Royal Western Yacht Club, Plymouth. A few days after his win he applied for Out Port membership of the Fowey Yacht Club. He and two other competing yacht owners who also applied were later elected members of the club.

In November 1894 the committee authorised Mr G S Treffry to ask Mr Charles E Treffry, the Squire of Place, if he would grant a lease of the old club premises at No2 Dolphin Square. This was agreed to, a long lease at £25 per annum. As no site for a new club was available it was agreed to improve the old club premises. The room above the smoking room was to become a card room and library and a new window was to be put in. It was also agreed that the WC by the quay doors should be

Canon Noel Purcell, vicar of St Fimbarrus Church for 55 years, 1867-1921. Brother-in-law of 'Squire' Charles Ebeneezer Treffry and an early member of the Fowey Yacht Club.

improved and that there should be two handwashing bowls to be emptied regularly, as the vicar had complained that they had been left full on two consecutive days.

As enthusiasm for the old premises revived the membership had increased so had income. It was resolved to buy new furniture for the new card room and to renovate and refurbish the dining room also.

After the death of Mrs Peard the housekeeper, in 1895, it was decided to advertise for a caretaker and to offer a salary of £25 as well as house rent. Mrs A Hodgeson was engaged at £20 per annum with house coals and lights. There were separate arrangements regarding her providing lunches and other refreshments.

Enthusiasm for a new club house continued and in April 1896 a possible site was under discussion. Mr W Gundry, a stockbroker of Torfrey near Golant, was the lessee of the site in a boatyard at the water's edge. He was invited to instruct his architect to prepare plans with reference to the requirements of the Fowey Yacht Club.

On June 2, 1896 the committee met Mr Gundry at a site meeting. He offered to put up a clubhouse according to the plan prepared by his architect, providing the cost did not exceed £600, at a rent of £40 per annum. If the cost of the building should exceed £600 the club should pay him 5% on the excess. Also, that the club should appoint trustees to be responsible for the payment of rent and that the lease should be drawn for a reasonable term. At a meeting later in the day it was resolved to decline Mr Gundry's offer as it involved possible expenses for which the club was not prepared to make itself liable. This must have been disappointing for everyone involved.

The committee temporarily abandoned the idea of a new clubhouse and once again discussed the possibilities of improving the present club premises at Dolphin House. At the AGM in November 1896 it was proposed that 20 £50 debentures bringing interest at 5% be issued to wipe off liabilities for decoration and enlargement of the present club premises.

In March 1897 it was reported to the committee that the District Council was prepared to allow the club to supply water to yachts for a fee of 5s per annum. It was decided to set up a hose and tap to carry the water down to the low water mark on the foreshore. It was also agreed to charge non-members for water but yachts belonging to club members should be supplied free of charge.

A FOWEY YACHT CLUB CELLAR LIST

OF 1897.

Champagnes

Moet 1892		7/6
" première cuvée		5/6
" 1889 half bottles		4/-
Louis Etienne		5/-
" " half bottles		2/9

Claret

St. Julien		2/6
" half bottles		1/6

Burgundy

Beaune & half bottles		1/9

Port

Crofts		5/-
" half bottles		2/9

Sherry

Gonzalez		4/-
" per glass		6ᵈ

Hock

Hockheimer 1886		3/6

Sherry & Bitters		6ᵈ per glass
Gin " "		3ᵈ " "
Chartreuse		6ᵈ " "
Kümmel		" " "
Liqueur Brandy		" " "
Whisky & Soda small		" " "
Brandy " " "		" " "

1

Queen Victoria's Diamond Jubilee, July 1 1897

Queen Victoria was 18 when she became Queen in 1837. Her Diamond Jubilee in 1897 celebrated 60 years on the throne. At a meeting at the club on May 12, 1897 it was decided to obtain a set of signal flags to decorate the club for Jubilee Day on July 1.

The previous month the Reverend Purcell, vicar of Fowey and a early member of the yacht club, had formally opened a new water reservoir to the town. The 300,000 gallon capacity reservoir was 75ft by 60ft, 11ft 6ins high and supported by strong pillars. The second reservoir soon to be finished at Windmill Field would add another 400,000 gallons thus at last ensuring an adequate supply of water. It was on Jubilee Day that Miss Purcell, daughter of the vicar, ceremonially turned on the water to the town.

Q had been deeply involved in the planning of Jubilee Day. He wrote:

"I worked the people up and we lined the streets with trees from end to end, put up arches and criss-crossed all between with lanterns and bunting till I had a mile of green bazaar, and we fed 1850 handsomely by the waterside, and marched and counter-marched by hundreds in fancy dress, till the gunpowder ran out of the heels of our boots."

"The local band under our windows roused us out at 7.00am and we crept to bed at 3.00am. In short sir the place went off its head and we hadn't a man drunk; a few merry but not what you may call drunk"

The Western Morning News of the time completes the account:

"The days proceedings opened with the ringing of bells after which a procession of Naval Reserves, Volunteers, Foresters, Oddfellows and Sunday School children marched through the town to the Town Quay where the Volunteers fired a "feu de joie" (a gun salute) and the National Anthem was sung. A special committee catered for the sailors in port, giving them a free tea at the Sailors Rest. There were boat races, sports on the cricket field and a grand fancy dress carnival in the evening. The proceedings concluded with a fancy dress ball in the Institute Hall and Town Hall."

The trees and foliage had been

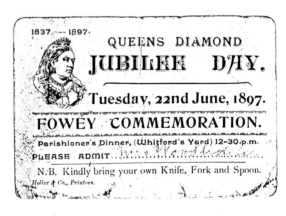

This ticket admitted Mrs Woodhouse to the parishioners dinner in Whitfords yard.
It was to be the site of the new yacht clubhouse built the following year.

39

Queen Victoria's Diamond Jubilee, July 1 1897. "A mile of green bazaar."

provided by Mr Treffry. One thousand parishioners sat down to lunch under an awning in Whitford's Yard and the fancy dress ball continued "with spirit" until 4am.

Somewhere around this time amidst the excitement and goodwill Mr Gundry verbally amended his offer of June 2 1896. It is not clear what were the amendments, but on August 10, 1897 on the eve of the regatta, it was agreed unanimously "that the select committee be instructed to endeavour to arrange with Mr Gundry for the erection by him of a suitable clubhouse, and for a lease of 21 years with breaks at 7 and 14 years, at a rent not exceeding £45, with covenants permitting use of the premises for any unobjectionable purpose in the event of the club ceasing to occupy them."

Fowey Royal Regatta 1897

Fowey Royal Regatta Day in 1897 was held on August 11. The Western Morning News reports:

"Fine weather favoured Fowey Royal Regatta yesterday. Up to noon the fate of the elements hung in the balance, when a couple of smart showers impressed many that the remainder of the day would be spent in mud, misery and mackintosh."

The newspaper reports continues:

"The afternoon however turned out beautifully fine and it would be difficult to imagine a prettier sight than was presented to the visitor in the compact and safe little harbour. Some fifty merchant ships, graceful yachts and trading boats were freely bedecked with bunting. Streamers and excursion trains from Plymouth, Looe and Falmouth brought hundreds of excursionists into the town and perhaps the only disappointing feature about the whole affair was that they were obliged to leave before the evening's attractions commenced."

"There was a good westerly breeze blowing and the yacht racing was consequently very good. Several noted Plymouth yachts took part in the matches promoted by the Fowey Yacht Club, having reached the port by taking part in the Channel race from Plymouth to Fowey on Tuesday.

"The courses laid down for the yachts could easily be commanded from the surrounding heights and large numbers of people witnessed the events from the shore with manifest interest".

"The church bells rang merry peals throughout the day and the quaint old town was filled with happy faces. There were steam horses (roundabouts) on the Town Quay and the band played, adding to the brightness of the scene. In the evening there was a water carnival and a grand display of fireworks from a vessel moored in mid harbour. The set piece of fireworks was a yawl yacht in full sail, the Cornish Arms and "Goodnight."

As usual there was a rush of new members eager to join the club following the pleasures of the regatta. Q had had an exhausting time of it and on September 25 he wrote that he was compelled to resign as Honorary Secretary of the club as he could no longer devote sufficient time to the duties.

Until this point the minutes of every meeting for the previous four years had been in his own meticulous handwriting. He had worked diligently for the club and it was the right time to resign from this onerous post. He had done a good job. The regatta had been yet another success and the plans for the new club were firmly established. Mr Hayton took on the job of Honorary Secretary and Q officially resigned ten days after. William Gundry of Torfrey died on September 20 at the age of 77, but the plans for the new clubhouse continued.

PROGRAMME

OF

FOWEY ROYAL

REGATTA

The Fowey Royal Regatta predates the foundation of the Fowey Yacht Club. The prefix Royal probably was adopted when royalty visited the town regatta.

Wednesday, 11th August, 1897.

President:-

E. ATKINSON, Esq.

Vice Presidents:-
A. T. QUILLER COUCH, Esq.
G. B. DAUNT, Esq.   Major EDWARDS,
Lieut HELBY, R.N.   L. S. LONG, Esq.,
Rev H. N. PURCELL, H. F. HAYTON Esq
A. M. SIMON, Esq.,   E. TREFFRY, Esq

Hon. Treas   Hon. Sec.
S. GALE,   W. H. WATTY.

HELLER & CO., MACHINE PRINTERS, FOWEY.

X 908/2

42

PROGRAMME.

Fowey Yacht Club Cup

Start 10 a.m.

A Handicap Race for Yachts above 10 and not exceeding 40 tons Thames Measurement. Course about 27 miles. First Prize a Silver Cup, value 20 Guineas (Presented by C. P. JOHNSON, Esq. Vice Commodore F.Y.C.) Second, 5 Guineas, Third, 3 Guineas. Entrance Fee, 15/-

1.	Moonbeam	Cutter 76 T.M.	C. P. Johnson, Esq.	Blue, White crescent
2.	Xanthe	" 18 "	A. M. Channing Esq &c.	White, Blue X
3.	Malcel	" 15 "	W. S. Kelly, Esq.	Blue, White Fleur-de-lys
4.	Hoopoe	" 20 "	K. S. Knapman Esq.	Red, White H
5.	Spinaway	" 20 "	W. H. Lean Esq.	Wht. Red Maltese cross
6.	Evig	" 90 "	H. R. A. K. St. Severin Esq	Blue, White St. Georges cross
7.	Winnie	" 21 "	E. W. Williamson Esq	Blue White Unicorn
8.	Florence		F M E Coath Allami Esq	Blue and yellow flag

HANDICAP.

Hoopoe Scratch. Spinaway 15'. Mabel 16'. Xanthe 18'. Winnie 20'. Moonbeam 22'. Florence 27'. Erig 31'.

The Commodore's Cup

A Handicap Race for Yachts not exceeding 10 Tons Thames Measurement. Course about 18 miles. First Prize, 10 Guineas (Presented by E. ATKINSON, Esq., Commodore F.Y.C.) Second, 4 Guineas. Third, 2 Guineas Entrance Fee, 10/-

1.	Stork	Cutter 6 T M	Major C. B. G. Dick, n.m.l.i.	Red, buff, blue horizontal
2.	Jilt	" 6 "	Dr C. Mouro Grier	Red, Red crescent
3.	Vida	" 6 "	A. T. Quiller-Couch, Esq	Orange, black horizontal black centre
4.	Fiera	" 6 "	Capt. J. Holditch	Orange, black S. Andrews cross
5.	Foam	" 6 "	Major A Salmon	Maroon, Yellow horizontal
6.	Cheer oh	" 6 "	C. W Polkinghorne Esq	Yellow, with Black bull
7.	Zoe	Yawl 3 "	Capt H Pursel Esq	Blue White Diagonal
8.	Cora	" "	G. B Daunt, Esq	Blue Peter
9.	Cora	Cutter 4 "	Capt A G Inglis	Red cross
10.	Volador	" 7 "	J F H Iles	Red and white horizontal
11.	Asthore	" 7 "	Dr F F' H Harden	Blue, Red cross
12.	Senta	" 7 "	J Cavander Esq	Dark blue and white diagonal
13.	Bessie	" 7 "	J E Cooper, Esq	Yellow, blue and white diagonal

Volador Scratch. Stork & Fiera 4'. Asthore 5'. Jilt 7'. Foam, Venus & Senta 9'. Cheer Oh 10'. Cora 11'. Zoe 14'. Bessie 15'.

For Yachts not exceeding 24 L.R.

Start 10-30 a.m.

A Race with Y.R.A. time allowance. Course about 12 miles First Prize, A Water Colour Drawing Presented by P. FLETCHER WATSON, Esq., and £5. Second, £2. Third, £1. Entrance Fee, 5/- The above Races to be Sailed under Y.R.A. Rules, and under control of the Regatta Committee of the Fowey Yacht Club.

1	Red Heart	Lugger 24ft L.a	H S Tuke Esq	White and Red chequers
2	Vendetta	" 17.46	Evelyn Simpson Esq	Black three red gutta
3	Centipede	" lift "	Tucker Esq	Blue and Yellow Diagonal
4	Dabdalai	" 34 "	H Blight Esq	

For Pleasure Yachts

A Handicap Race for Yachts under 20 tons belonging to the Port of Fowey but not owned by members of recognised Yacht Clubs. Flying start from Committee Ship. No Ballast to be shifted. First Prize, £3. Second, £2. Third, £1. Entrance Fee, 2/6.

SAILING BOATS

Start at 11 a.m. Not exceeding 18ft Overall. First Prize, A Challenge Cup and £3. Second, £2. Third, £1. Entrance Fee, 1/-

SAILING BOATS

Start at 11-15. Not exceeding 16ft Overall. First Prize, £2 10/- Second, £1 5/- Third, 15/- Fourth, 7/6 Entrance Fee, 1/-

MOSQUITO FLEET OF SAILING BOATS

Start at 11-30. Not exceeding, 15ft overall. First Prize £1 10s. Second, £1. Third, 10s. Entrance Fee, 1/-

YACHTS PUNTS

Start at 12 noon. Not exceeding 12ft. 6ins. overall. First Prize 10/- Second, 7/6. Third 5/- Entrance Fee, 1/-

Four-Oared Gigs & Whale Boats

Start at 2 p.m. Belonging to H.M.S. To be pulled by Coast Guard Men of Fowey Division. First Prize, £2 10/- First Prize £1 10/- Third, £1. Entrance Fee 1/-

Four-Oared Merchant Ships Boats

Start at 2-15. Not exceeding 17ft. by not less than 5ft 6ins. beam, First Prize, £2. Second, £1 5/- Third, 10/- Entrance Fee, 1/-

H.M.S. Four-Oared Gigs

Start at 2-30. To be pulled by Lads under 18 years of Age. First Prize, £1 10/- Second, £1 Third, 10/- Fourth, 5/- Entrance Fee, 1/-

SINGLE PADDLING RACE

Start at 2-45. Not exceeding 16ft by not less than 4ft 6ins. beam. First Prize, 15/- Second, 10/- Third, 5/- Entrance Fee, 1/-

LADIES RACE

Start at 3. Timepiece. Silver Mounted Umbrella. Brass Fire Set. Silver Brooch. The winner to have the choice of either of these articles.

Four-Oared Merchant Ships Boats

Start at 3-30. To be pulled by Lads under 16 years of Age. First Prize, £1 Second, 15/- Third, 10/- Fourth, 5/- Entrance Fee, 1/-

Two-Oared Boats

Start at 3-45. Not exceeding 15ft 6ins by not less than 4ft 6ins beam. First Prize, £1. Second, 12/6 Third, 7/6. Entrance Fee, 1/-

Two-Oared Race with Coxswain

Start at 4. To be pulled by Boys under 14 years of Age In Boats not exceeding 15ft by not less than 4ft 6ins beam. First Prize, 15/- Second, 10/- Third, 5/-

RAN-DAN RACE

Start at 4-30. In Boats not exceeding 15ft 6ins. by not less than 4ft. 6ins beam. First Prize, £1. Second, £1 Third, 15/- Entrance Fee, 1/-

A Swimming Match

Start at 5 p.m. For Lads under 20 years of Age. Distance 500 yards. First Prize, £1. Second, 10- Third, 7/6 Fourth, 5/-

A SWIMMING MATCH

Start at 5-15. For Lads under 16 years of Age. Distance 200 Yards. First Prize, 12/6 Second, 7/6 Third, 5/- Fourth, 2/6

A Swimming Match

Start at 5-30. For Boys under 14 years of Age. Distance 100 yards. First Prize, 10/- Second, 7/6 Third, 5/- Fourth, 2/6

Walking the Greasy Pole for a Pig.

A GRAND DISPLAY OF FIREWORKS

Will take place at 9 o'clock (Weather Permitting) when the following Prizes will be offered for Illuminated Yachts and Boats.

For the best Illuminated Yacht, First Prize, £10 Second, £4. For the best Illuminated Boat, First Prize, £3. Second, £1 10/- Third, £1,

In addition to which there will be a Special Prize offered for the Boat Illuminated in the most novel design. Four Yachts or Boats to compete or no Second Prize, Three to compete or no First Prize,

The Illuminated Boats taking part in the Water Carnival are to be alongside the Committee Ship fully Illuminated at 9-30 at which hour the Steamer will start towing the Procession. Only boats taking part in the Procession will be eligible to compete.

SPECIAL PRIZES

Offered for

FLORAL DECORATED BOATS

£5. Will be divided, according to taste and originality, to the Boats Best Decorated with wild Flowers, Grasses &c. *No paper to be used.* Due allowance will be made to Children who Decorate their Boats themselves.

£1. Prize for the best Adult Darky Party, *with permission to collect.*

10s. Prize for the best Boys Darky Party do.

5s. Additional will be given to Darky Party with the best Floral Decorated Boat.

All competing boats to assemble between White House and Castle Ruins at 2-30 p.m., sharp, where Entries will be received by Mr., J. M. CLEMENS.

Competitors to remain about the Harbour during the Regatta Prizes will l e distributed at 6 p.m. at the assembling place

The awards of Committee to be final.

J. D. MAIER, Hon. Sec.

Carnival Committee.

Q continued as a committee member. He was now 33 years of age. One week later the Annual General Meeting was held. It was reported that there were now 87 club members on the books and 17 of those had been elected during the year 1897. Twelve members had resigned or been expunged for non-payment. The tonnage of yachts was 1,702 tons.

It was agreed that in order to furnish the new club money should be raised by the issue of £5 debentures. Nine members guaranteed £250. Ten debentures at £5 were taken up by the Commodore, Edward Atkinson, the other members each taking half that number.

The Commodore, whom everyone called Atky, was re-elected. Mr C P Johnson was re-elected Vice-Commodore. For the first time there was to be a Rear Commodore, and Q was elected to this post. He was proposed by the vicar and seconded by Mr Phelps.

Four days later at a special meeting a new member was elected unanimously. He was William Gundry Mills, a stockbroker of Regents Park, London. He was an executor of the will of Mr William Gundry. The other executor was Thomas Gundry, already a member of the club.

Discussions with the architect continued, regarding the specifications for the new club. The project was made public in the following announcement: "The members of the Fowey Yacht Club have decided to build a new clubhouse in a good position and expect to have it ready for occupation in the spring. This new departure will assuredly be appreciated by yachting men, for Fowey, a favourite half-way house 'twixt Plymouth and Falmouth, is altogether a charming little port and easy to negotiate, both in and out. Dredging operations for its further improvement are in progress under the supervision of the Harbour Commissioners, so that any further determination of the club to make it the best yacht club west of Plymouth is commendable, and will doubtless meet with the success it deserves. The total of the club boats is close upon 2,000 tons, and new members are, we understand, coming in so rapidly as to justify the little talk there already is of clapping on an entrance fee in the near future."

The Rt. Hon Leonard Courtney MP for Bodmin Division was unanimously elected to honorary membership meaning that he paid no fees. His gracious letter of acceptance was written on October 31, 1897 on Fowey Hotel notepaper.

Advertisements inviting tenders for the building of the new clubhouse were placed in the Western Morning News and the Western Daily Mercury. Four builders responded and the lowest tender was accepted. It was unanimously decided that Messrs Blamey and Hoskins be engaged. Their estimate was for £830 to erect the building and roof it with slates. A tile roof would have cost £36 more. The tenders were received in December 1897 and the building was ready for use eight months later.

Seventeen members agreed to act as guarantors regarding payment of rent. The lessors objected to this cumbersome arrangement and so it was agreed that the flag officers should be guarantors under an indemnity from the members on behalf of the club. It was arranged that the club should open on August 9, 1898.

It was a considerable advantage to the town of Fowey when the yacht club was established on such a sound footing as that in 1898. The town's economy had been in decline for some time. The ship building yards had stopped building cargo carriers. Steam was replacing sail and it was large ships that were now in demand and these were made elsewhere. The old shipwright skills were no longer in demand and there was much unemployment. The fishing industry had declined and was unpredictable. Tin and copper mining had moved away from the area. In 1898 Q was pressing for the development of the tourist industry to bring back a measure of prosperity to Fowey. He said: "Were it within human capacity to decide between revival of our ancient industries, fishery and mining, and the development of new business our decision would be prompt enough. But it is not. Well then, since we must cater for the stranger, let us do it well and honestly. Let us respect him and our native land as well."

There had been many changes in the town. Old, dilapidated cob buildings were replaced with new buildings of granite or brick. Beyond Whitehouse slip there was much building of private houses, hotels and boarding houses. The railway brought families of holidaymakers who would spend the summer in the newly-built villas of Fowey. Most householders employed domestic help, housekeepers, cooks, maids, cleaners and laundry workers. Holiday yachting brought employment also. Skippers and paid hands were important for their energy and skills. Yachting folk employed them as crew. They often wore uniforms provided by their employers, jerseys with the name of the yacht owner's boat embroidered conspicuously, and sometimes also a reefer jacket. Their local knowledge of tides and windshifts were invaluable as well as the finer points of sailing. And when the wind died it was the paid hands who would toil over the long sweeps as they rowed back to port.

As tourism developed the town enjoyed a degree of prosperity. The decline that William Rashleigh had deplored 30 years previously had begun to reverse and slowly optimism and employment returned to the town.

"And the band played ..."
Regatta in the harbour of Fowey. In the foreground on a hull boarded with planks is a 20 piece military band. They have forms to sit upon and a string of Chinese lanterns overhead.

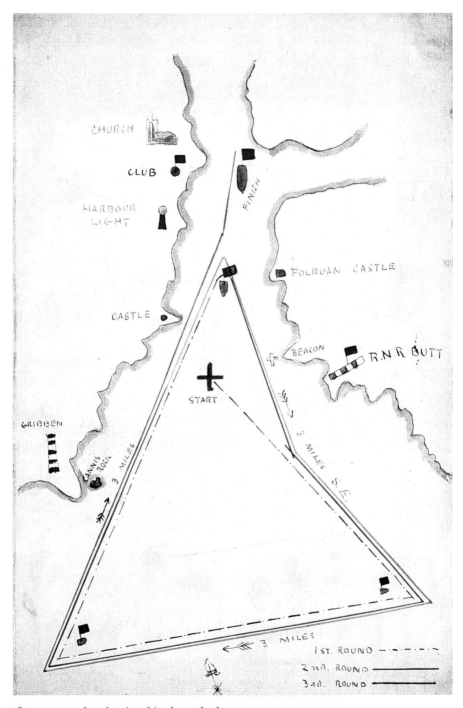

Courses were hand-painted in the early days.

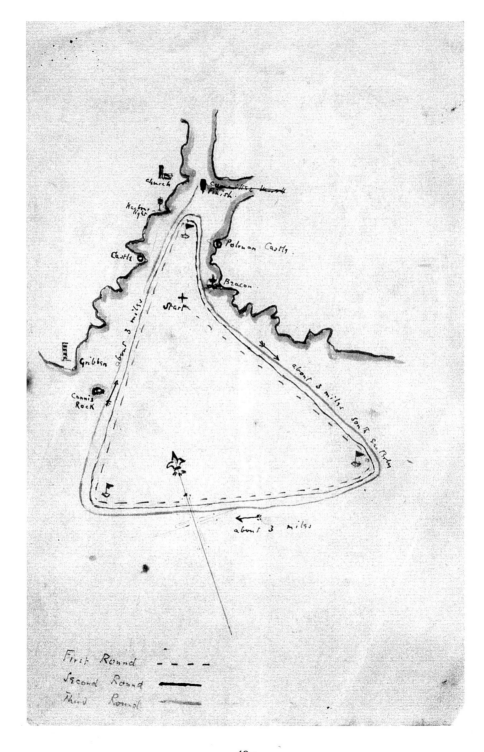

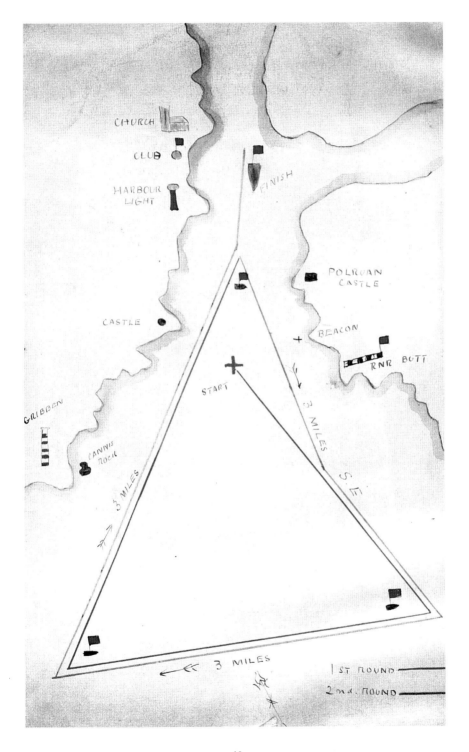

Arthur Thomas Quiller-Couch otherwise Q

Arthur was born on November 21st 1863 at No 63 Fore Street, Bodmin where his father was a doctor. He was the eldest of five children and first went to school in Bodmin. Arthur's mother Mary was from Devon and it was from his grandparents home in Abbotskerswell that he attended Newton Abbot College. After two years as a day boy he boarded at school.

His holidays were spent in Bodmin with his parents and from there he explored the surrounding countryside.

Q first came to Fowey in his teens for the benefit of sea air as he was said to have outgrown his strength. The year was 1879. He had lodgings above the Old Post Office but the room overlooked the street so he found another room in an attic with a window that looked out over the harbour. He later wrote the following:

> "That night before undressing I stood long and gazed on the harbour, the track of the moon on its water, the riding lights of two or three small schooners at anchor in the shadow of the farther shore, and decided that this were no bad place in which to live. And that is all I need to say here of my first acquaintance with the upper and lower reaches of an estuary, the tide of which time has woven so close into the pulse of my own life that memory cannot now separate the rhythms."

It was love at first sight and his delight in Fowey and the harbour persisted throughout his life.

Arthur's father Thomas Couch found the financial burden of educating his five children difficult. Arthur was encouraged to try for a scholarship. He was successful and won a place at Clifton College in Bristol. He was resident there from the age of 17 until 1882 when he won an entrance scholarship in Classics at Trinity College, Oxford.

At the beginning of Q's third year at Trinity College, Oxford his father died. He left no provision for his widow and children. It seemed that Q as the eldest son would have to abandon his studies and get a job in order to support his mother and siblings. However, his grandfather Elias Ford agreed to help and so Q was able to complete his education.

Q hoped to achieve good results in his final examinations. If he were awarded a first class degree he would be elected a Fellow of the College with a chance of an academic career and staying in Oxford for good. However, in 1896 he was disappointed that after sitting his final examinations he was only awarded a second class degree. The President and Fellows of Trinity College appointed him to a college lectureship but the future was not as promising as he had hoped.

Q's father had left many debts behind after his death. Soon after completing his studies Elias Ford sent for Q in Plymouth to discuss "serious business." It was indeed serious. Elias Ford had lost the residue of his estate attempting to rescue his elder brother's fortunes from shipwreck. He was no longer able to support his daughter and her family. The responsibility for the financial care of his mother, two sisters and two brothers (still schoolboys) fell upon Q.

Q felt guilty that his disappointing examination results had not secured the family's future. He vowed not only to support them but to pay off his father's debts as well. He wrote: "I had provided myself in Mr Thornton's shop across the High Street with a few steel nibs and a cork penholder costing just two pence or two pence half penny. He said: "Well you and I have just made a mess of things. So it's for you and me together to make amends." With this same penholder I have written all my stories, essays, lectures, verse etc. as with it I am writing this page fifty odd years later."

He wrote prodigiously, supplementing his income by working as a tutor during vacations. Lord Leconfield at Petworth engaged him as classics tutor to his eldest son. It was during this vacation that he began to write his first novel 'Dead Man's Rock.'

Whenever he could he returned to Fowey and spent part of every summer there. He had met Miss Louisa Amelia Hicks very early on. She lived in a house in North

The Haven, home of Sir Arthur and Lady Quiller-Couch. Notice the flag pole where news of election results were conveyed to the town. Q and his young wife Louie and baby son Bevil moved to the Haven in 1892. At first they rented the house which had been built for a retired sea captain. Later Q was able to buy the property which remained the family home for the rest of their lives

Lady Quiller-Couch outside the Haven with staff.

Street, Fowey with her elder sister Jane Ann Hicks and her mother Ann Hicks who was the widow of a sea captain.

The same evening as the fateful meeting with Elias Ford in Plymouth in 1896 Q returned to Fowey and proposed marriage to Louisa.

Fifty years later Q wrote in 'Memories and Opinions':

"I declare that hour the most fortunate of my life. We had halted half way in a short lane leading up from the sea and beside a low wall coped by a quantity of wild thyme, on a tuft of which I rested my hand as I spoke and waited for her answer. To this day, halting before a tuft of the plant I press it and recall that answer in its fragrance."

But marriage had to wait until he had paid off the family debts.

In 1887 he moved to London, convinced he could make money as a famous writer. For six years he worked night and day writing articles, short stories and poems for various Fleet Street publications. By the time he was 25 he had written three novels. In 1888 his novel 'The Astonishing History of Troy Town' was published by Cassells, a thinly disguised account of life in Fowey.

The following year on August 22, 1889 he and Louisa were married in St Fimbarrus Church, Fowey. For a while they lived in London, but Louisa did not settle and returned to her mother's home when she became pregnant. Their son Bevil was born in October 1890. Q was seriously overworked and in the autumn of 1891 had a breakdown and was advised to leave London. He suffered from insomnia, developed a nervous fear of crowds and was fearful of crossing the street. They returned to Fowey, at first living in a small house that was later converted into a boot shop. In 1892 the little family moved to the Haven, which they rented. Years later Q was able to buy the house and it remained their home for the rest of their lives.

Q had made many friends in London who must have been sad to see him leave, but the friendships persisted and many were welcome visitors to his home at the Haven. He became well known and popular in Fowey.

Edward Atkinson - The First Commodore

The closest of Q's many friends in Fowey was Edward Atkinson, the Commodore of the yacht club. He was known to all as Atky. He was 30 years older than Q and in his early fifties when the Quiller-Couchs finally settled in Fowey. He had never married. Atky had been born in Highgate, London to a wealthy family who were the manufacturers of Atkinsons Lavender Perfume. He went to Highgate Grammar School but finished his education in Paris. He was a keen balloonist and made various ascents with balloonists of the time.

He was also a keen canoeist, starting with the early Rob Roy canoes. These were developed in Scotland by a man called McGregor who devised canoes with decking and sails. Atky was a pioneer of these canoes. He made one voyage from the Thames to Torbay during which he capsized and

Edward Atkinson

was in the water for two hours. He almost drowned. Another feat of daring was an epic voyage around Cape Wrath and the North coast of Scotland in a small dug-out canoe.

By 1880 he had made his home at Rosebank, Mixtow Creek which became a popular venue for many visitors. He had a large picture gallery with drawings by Turner and Vonnington. It was Atky's pleasure to entertain his friends and visitors.

There were various people who attended him. Most notable was Miss Kate Isabel Marston, his cousin and housekeeper. She would prepare wonderful cream teas for those who visited the house to admire the objets d'art and pictures that Atky collected. Atky had a passion for mechanical toys of all kinds and the drawers in his home were filled with them. Kenneth Grahame was included in a boat trip up river with Q. He wrote to his fiancée, Elspeth Thompson in baby talk: "We found a drore full of toys wot wound up, and we ad a great race between a fish, a snaik, a beetle wot flapped its wings and a rabbit."

Atky could afford to indulge his pleasures and eccentricities. He was a wealthy man who wore exquisite and idiosyncratic hats which he ordered from Paris. It is unlikely that Miss Marston ever visited the upper floor of Rosebank. There was no staircase to the bedroom which was reached instead by a rope ladder. Apparently in his youth Atky was an amateur chemist and was a friend of Faraday and Tyndall. He was a collector of books and a lover of good literature, especially of poetry. He had an especial knack of making friends with men younger than himself. Amongst them were Kenneth Grahame, Hillaire Belloc and G K Chesterton.

Th River Fowey at Mixtow, 1889. The home of Commodore Atkinson at Mixtow Creek to the right of the picture. At the jetty a steamer SS Clio *is being loaded with china clay from railway wagons. Sailing vessels are moored midstream.*

Mr Edward Atkinson and his cousin Miss Kate Isabel Marston being rowed between their home at Mixtow, and Fowey.

Atky occasionally took undergraduate friends on canoeing trips in the South of France. His enduring passion was messing about in boats. He owned more than 30 different craft, each of which had its own history in connection with his adventures. They were kept in several boat houses at Mixtow.

Airymouse was his favourite boat. Atky had engaged a Mr Edwin Brett to design her and she had been built by William H Watty in Fowey. She was built as a cutter, 58 feet length overall, and was two years in the making.

Airymouse is the Cornish name for a bat and the boat had a figurehead of a bat modelled by a Mr Calcott. It was cast in gilt bronze by Broad and Sons in London.

'Airymouse' was launched on July 12, 1894. The Cornwall Gazette reported:

"All Fowey and its many visitors seemed afloat on Thursday evening to witness the launch of a yacht built by Mr Watty for Mr Edward Atkinson. As she dipped in the water with a fall of a few feet she shipped a large quantity of water and all on board were swamped. Two pleasure boats got under her stern but fortunately no accident happened. Fowey Town Band under Mr W Hawken played selections. Mr Watty was heartily congratulated on turning out so beautiful a vessel".

Airymouse, *built in 1894 for Commodore Edward Atkinson.*

The new Yacht Club

News of the building of the new yacht club appeared in the March 5 1898 issue of the Western Morning News. This was a rearrangement of the previous years piece when Q was still Hon. Sec.:

"Frequenters of the South coast will learn with appreciation that the Fowey Yacht club are erecting a new clubhouse which will be a large building replete with modern comforts and containing smoking, billiard and dining rooms. Mr A Quiller-Couch, the energetic secretary, is doing everything in his power to make the beautiful little harbour more popular as a cruising and racing resort.

"Lying as it does in the bight of the bay, Fowey is practically a blind harbour and many a yachtsman has passed up the coast from Falmouth to Plymouth in dirty weather without being aware of the fact that such a snug anchorage as Fowey existed. The once famous trading post is gradually coming into prominence among yachtsmen and the energetic yacht club has done, and is continuing to do, much in the way of organising regattas.

"There are now over 100 members who own between them over 2,000 yacht tons and it is said that so many candidates are coming up for election that it will not be very long before an entrance fee is charged to Out Port members as is now done for residents.

"Fowey being what one might term a half way house between Plymouth and Falmouth is a convenient and charming port of call for yachts. Dredging operations will be recommended almost immediately.

There is some talk amongst the members of the club forming a small boat racing class after the style of the Teignmouth class."

The opening of the new clubhouse was celebrated on August 9, 1898. The Royal Cornwall Gazette on August 11, 1898 reported:

"Tuesday last, the first of our two-day royal Regatta will long be remembered as the day on which the yacht club's new clubhouse was opened. The building itself is most picturesque and is built on ground where, for a time, a shed for building yachts stood. The view from the club grounds is very lovely and commands a view of the entrance to the harbour. The flag officers and members of the club celebrated the opening of their new clubhouse by giving a reception on Tuesday afternoon. The weather was all that could be desired; the reception was a brilliant function and the invitations given by the club resulted in the assembling of about two hundred guests. The band of the Royal Marines was in attendance and a most eloquent and sumptuous afternoon tea was provided by the hosts. The tea was held in the fine billiard room and the clubhouse itself was thrown open to the guests. A crimson and white awning was erected along the whole length of the building and seats were placed under it.

"In the evening we had a carnival and a feast of lanterns. A great many houses

The new Royal Fowey Yacht Club built 1898 and is little changed today.

along the route were illuminated and the effect was charming.

"After the carnival a fancy dress ball took place in the Albert Hall. All of those who had worked so hard to establish the club in new premises must have been well satisfied. The weather had been perfect and both the sailing and the social scene had been well supported."

The August regatta had been an enjoyable success.

At a meeting of the committee in October 1898 it was reported that the membership had rapidly risen from 130 to 167. There were 37 new members. Committee meetings had been conducted smoothly and the only contentious issues being the institution of a one shilling fine for sitting on the billiard table and also fines of two shillings and sixpence for members who remained in the club after the time call at 11.55pm. There was harmony with minor indiscretions being met with expectations of protocol and disciplinary measures in the form of fines.

It is interesting to record the comments of the Reverend Purcell during the first winter in the new club. He wrote in the suggestions book: "Could we have 2 or 3 small lamps in the reading room so that it would be possible to light one or more when members wish to read the papers after sunset. I find it very difficult to read there now unless I stand directly under the gas."

The Honorary Secretary responded: "There are already two candlesticks provided. Perhaps the member would present the club with what he requires."

The vicar seems to have been somewhat nettled. He replied: "Is it not a little rough on a member who asked for more light to be virtually told "provide it yourself"?! If the finances of our club won't run to a hand lamp or two or a few candlesticks even (so as not to rob the writing tables of necessary lights) I will with pleasure do what H H suggests and present a lamp or two, say at 1s 4d each. I would first try and improve the illuminating however of the gas lamp by providing white shades instead of yellow ones."

The Reverend Purcell had been vicar of Fowey since 1867. He was married to Anne Ellen Treffry, the eldest daughter of the Reverend Edward John Treffry. His father-in-law had inherited Place in 1850 and became vicar of Fowey in January 1863. Four years later he resigned in favour of his son-in-law who remained vicar of Fowey for 54 years. He died in 1921. The Reverend Purcell and his wife had four sons and three daughters. Anne Ellen died at the vicarage on March 5, 1877. She was just 37 years of age. By the time he complained about the reading lamps he had been a widower for 21 years.

The Reverend Purcell does not seem to have been a sailing man but appears to have used the club a great deal for letter writing and consulting reference books and reading newspapers.

By the AGM on November 29, 1899 membership had risen to 206 and the yacht tonnage was 3,070.

It was resolved that there should be cards left on visiting yachts indicating that

"The flag officers and members of the Fowey Yacht Club desire to offer the use of their club to owners of yacht . . . . . (name of visiting yacht) and his friends during their stay in port."

On a more mundane level at the same meeting, a letter from Mrs Hunkin was read which stated that she had arranged not to dry her washing in front of her house and alleging that members caused annoyance to her by looking in at her windows and making uncomplimentary remarks. It was decided to raise the matter amongst the members and no further complaints were recorded.

The suggestions book continued to provide colourful impressions of life in the club and the ever-present problem of getting there. Some members who lived close by walked to the club. Many Out Port members arrived by boat from their holiday yachts. There was limited car parking in the early days of motor cars. However, an unexpected solution was indicated by the following plaintive entry of July 28, 1900: "I beg to suggest that some accommodation be provided for bicycles."

The greatest number of complaints at this time refer to the lavatories:

"I suggest that clean towels be placed in the lavatory more frequently." C Jones, March 30, 1899

"A door silencer on the lavatory door would be a boon - expense not great." W Grahame, July 7, 1900.

"That the lavatory accommodation is insufficient and causes great inconvenience to members." Four members including local GP. August 1901.

Dr Sydney Morse was a very vociferous member of the club. He must have joined at the end of 1900 and was living at the time in Bagatelle House in Fowey. He was the member who was summoned to a special committee meeting for refusing to pay fines for after hours drinking in the club.

Of the suggestions made to the committee during the next eight years, nearly a quarter of them - 17 in number - were made by Dr Morse. Some were constructive, others critical. He requested that the club take on a Sporting Daily paper during the flat-racing and cricket season. He requested that two pairs of hairbrushes be kept in the lavatory, a wet and a dry pair. In 1910 he suggested that the speaking tubes in the club were unsanitary and unsatisfactory and should be replaced with electric bells. The last suggestion that he made to the committee was in 1910.

Temporary membership of the yacht club was a straightforward matter: two shillings for three days membership, three shillings and six pence for a week and ten shillings for a month.

By now Q was established in the community of the town. He and Louisa Hicks had been married on August 22, 1889 in St Fimbarrus Church, Fowey when Q was 25 years of age and Louisa 28. Louisa's mother had not approved of her future son-in-law. Perhaps the fact that he toiled throughout the long engagement to pay off family debts worried Mrs Hicks. How would her daughter manage being married to a penniless writer? She need not have worried. Ten years later Q was making a success of life in Fowey.

Q remained in touch with his old journalist friends in London. The railway journey from Paddington to Fowey was uncomplicated and the route along the coast in the West was spectacular. Trains. at Caffa Mill were met by horse and carriage, some of them supplied by the Fowey Hotel Company and others privately owned. Guests would be met at the station and greatly surprised by Q's boisterous welcome to the town when he would be accompanied by clowns or girls in fancy dress, or the ubiquitous Town Band before conducting visitors to the Haven or the Fowey Hotel.

A handy little local cruiser

J.M. Barrie in Fowey

J M Barrie, an old colleague of Q, from their days when they both worked for The Speaker in London came to Fowey several times in the early days. Like so many others, he fell in love with the scene. He wrote:

> "It is but a toy town to look at on a bay so small, hemmed in so picturesquely by cliffs and ruins that of a moonlight night it might pass for a scene in a theatre."

After his marriage Barrie brought his wife Mary to Fowey and spent many hours with Q. He derived great pleasure from Bevil who was four years old at the time of the visit. He later wrote to Q: "He is my favourite boy in the wide, wide world." The marriage of Barrie and Mary the year before had not flourished. They arrived with luggage and notebooks, accompanied by

J.M. Barrie, author of Peter Pan

their dog Porthos, a St Bernard who was later the inspiration for Nana in the story of Peter Pan. Whilst on their honeymoon in Switzerland, as well as buying Porthos James Barrie had purchased a camera. With this he took many photographs of Bevil and the dog out walking together. He made a hand-written story book entitled 'The Pippa and Porthos.' It included 24 photographs of Bevil. he wrote on the cover "Dedicated to Mrs Quiller-Couch (without her permission) January 1895. It was not intended for publication but as a gift for Bevil and his parents. Although Barrie remained Q's friend, regularly sent Christmas presents to Bevil and became a proxy godparent to Q's daughter Foy, he never visited Fowey again.

Barrie later became a well-known playwright and was a constant visitor to the home of Gerald du Maurier who was an actor manager in London. Daphne du Maurier regarded him as an uncle. It is possible that Barrie's enthusiasm for Q and Fowey encouraged the family to visit the place themselves.

Mary, his wife

Kenneth Grahame in Fowey

Another visitor was Kenneth Grahame. He was aged 40 and a published writer when he first visited Fowey. He was convalescing from a serious lung condition and came to the town to aid his recuperation. He stayed in the Fowey Hotel which he found a charming place with a "nice, narrow bed." Kenneth Grahame wrote: "as the river mouth came in view last night, with the boats and the little grey town I felt somehow as if I was coming home."

Kenneth Grahame in Fowey

It was 1899 and he seemed to be pleased to be apart from his fiancée, Elspeth Thompson. She was a spinster age 36, verging on "middle age" in those days. Bachelors had fought shy of her and she pursued Kenneth relentlessly. He wrote to her in baby talk, calling her by the name of whatever boat took his fancy in Fowey Harbour, 'Kiwi', 'Silverseas', 'Dashing Wave' and 'Nanny.'

Soon after his arrival Kenneth Grahame was introduced to Q. They became friends instantly and Q took great pleasure in introducing him to the boating fraternity. He quickly took to Atky as he shared Kenneth Grahame's passion for mechanical toys. Drawers and cupboards in his house at Mixtow were packed with them.

The friendship of Kenneth and Elspeth continued and was largely sustained by letters to each other, written in their curious baby talk. It is strange to consider that he was a successful businessman, 40 years of age, in a responsible job with the Bank of England.

At last, perhaps inspired by the happy family life of the Quiller-Couchs, he wrote to propose marriage. He told Elspeth that he took Q's advice and got in touch "with a tame curick" who would read the banns and conduct the service. The "tame curick" was of course the Reverend Purcell.

Three weeks later the couple were married on July 22 1899 at St Fimbarrus Church, Fowey. The bride did not wear the formal dress her sister had brought for her from London the day before. Instead she wore an old muslin dress that she had

Elspeth Thompson before her marriage to Kenneth Grahame. Painted by Sir Frank Dicksee.

worn for her early morning walk around St Catherine's headland with a slightly wilted daisy chain she had made for herself around her neck. Bevil and Foy were attendants at the wedding. Bevil looked especially fine in white satin breeches and a cocked hat.

The honeymoon lasted for three days in St Ives but Kenneth soon returned to Fowey and his boating friends. Elspeth was isolated at the Haven where she felt ill at ease. From the beginning she and Q had disliked each other. Nor did she like her husband's other close friend, Atky, whose company her husband seemed to prefer to that of her own.

Elspeth's excited courtship expectations came to nothing. Although she was quickly pregnant it was not a happy marriage. Kenneth, repelled by this adult relationship, retreated into his safe private world, in his own words: "a

Bevil dressed as a page for the wedding of Kenneth Grahame and Elspeth Grahame, July 22 1899. On the day he wore a bunch of roses in his button hole.

world clean of the clash of sex, a world of animals and Wind in the Willows."

Their only child Alastair was born on May 12, 1900. He was a sickly boy, physically handicapped and sensitive. He had a cataract and was blind in his right eye as well as having a squint. He was a disappointment to his parents who nicknamed him Mouse. In his absence Elspeth would try to convince others that he was brilliant.

He was frequently left in the care of domestic staff. In 1904 whilst Elspeth was taking a "cure" away from home, Kenneth Grahame and Atky set off for Paris together. Kenneth wrote to his wife in this customary "baby talk": which they had both used during their courtship by letter writing. Of the French trip Kenneth wrote:

"Atky behaving pretty well. You have an awful "down" on him but make no allowance for the tremendous convenience of having a man who's delighted to look up timetables, pay hotels and do all the tipping etc. etc."

It seems to have been a leisurely tour through France but the couple had to hurriedly return from Toulouse. Mouse was critically ill with peritonitis. It was a lengthy convalescence for the little boy who did survive the illness.

The relationship between Elspeth and Kenneth was not warm. They took holidays separately and Mouse was usually left behind.

Kenneth Grahame's rejection of his son was not as extreme as that of Elspeth. Mouse would be greatly comforted by bedtime stories when his father told him of the adventures of a badger, a mole, a toad and a water rat and the places they lived in, like the river bank in Lerryn Creek.

The Grahames came back to Fowey in 1907. Mouse was again left behind at home. Elspeth did not stay long and Kenneth Grahame took up with his friends Atky and Q again. The stories of the animals of the riverbank now reached Mouse in letters from his father, colourful accounts of the happiness of bachelor life in riverside homes and the pleasures of messing about in boats. 'Wind in the Willows' was published in October 1908 when the stories in the letters were linked in continuous narrative.

In the Spring of 1911 Kenneth Grahame came back to Fowey. He said: "I want Mouse to make the acquaintance of my Cornish haunts and friends before he goes to school." Alastair greatly enjoyed the holiday. The Commodore provided magnificent lunches at Rosebank, mostly fancy hors d'oevres and every sort of sausage, prepared by Mrs Marston. Atky allowed Mouse, now aged 11, to browse amongst his books and treasures.

Q took most of his guests to visit a small piece of land he had cultivated behind the old ale house Prime Cellars, at the water's edge close to Bodinnick. Q called it "The Farm" and believed that it was a relic of ancient ornamental gardens that zigzagged down from the Hall Walk. It had been created by the Mohans in 1600 to serve the mansion which once stood at Hall Farm. Q would row there daily when he was in Fowey in his bright red boat 'True Tilda' or the 'Picotee.' Kenneth Grahame wrote: "One sunny day we all went over there with a large luncheon basket and lunched in the open in a riot of daffodils and primroses with three big foreign ships, Danes and Norwegians, moored right below us."

Whenever people came to visit Q in Fowey the pattern seems to have been similar when a Dutch novelist called Maarten Maartens visited Fowey. He wrote to a friend:
"This is quite an exquisite place. Quiller-Couch and his home and his surroundings and family quite ideal. King of Fowey in a quiet way, and such a kingdom, with a delightful little yacht club next door for the civilised world to turn up in handy at tea time. What a good fortune to be born to!

"The day has been supremely enjoyable - an exquisite old church in the morning, on the bay and river all the afternoon, to a highly cultivated friend across the water with two rooms full of pictures."
The church was that of St Fimbarrus and the "highly cultivated friend" was Atky.

The Coronation of Edward VII

Q worked hard for the community as well as the yacht club. The coronation of Edward VII was planned for June 26, 1902. Queen Victoria had died the year before. As usual Q was in charge of the arrangements for the celebrations in the town. However, the King was ill and the festivities were delayed until the Saturday before the regatta.

On the morning of August 9 the town festivities commenced at 8am, with the ringing of the church bells. Then at 9am children assembled at the railway station to be presented with medals donated by C A Hanson Esq. The medals were distributed by Mrs Quiller-Couch and Mrs Hayton (another yacht club wife). Then at 9.30am a large procession led by the Fowey Artillery Volunteers marched to the church where Mrs Treffry and Mrs Purcell planted trees. There was a church service followed by a cannon salute from the town quay. Children's sports were followed by teas on the town quay.

Q and Foye standing outside the Haven decorated for the coronation of Edward VII, June 26 1902.

A second parade led by the band at 9pm was in fancy dress with participants carrying lanterns. The harbour was illuminated with coloured lights, as was the yacht club. Then at 10.30pm a fancy dress ball was held in the Town Hall and Working Men's Institute.

Q must have had a very busy day for at 6pm he was back in the yacht club presiding at a meeting of the sailing committee as the regatta was only a few days away. Fowey remained "en fete" and all the decorations remained until after the sailing races three days later.

Q was an admirable chairman; apparently keeping his committee always focused on the business in hand. It is clear that when personality clashes and crises occurred it always fell to Q to take the role of mediator, pouring calming oil on troubled water.

His sense of humour was also very marked. During his year of office as Mayor of Fowey it was recalled by a fellow councillor how he would sit in his chair with one eye on the clock and would chide the long-winded in a gracious manner in order to expedite business. Always the gentleman he was well known for his courtesy and humanity and wit.

When Q left Fleet Street it was because his health had broken down and he could no longer cope with the pressure of journalism in London, and frequent travel to see his family in Fowey. It was always a matter of anxiety to him whether he would be able to support his home and family from his writing. However he was diligent and wrote constantly.

Having always been a regular contributor to the magazine 'The Speaker' since his early days, he finally stopped submitting regular pieces. He started editing 'The Cornish Magazine' and by 1903 had published nine novels. He wrote many short stories. His idol was Robert Louis Stevenson who had left an unfinished novel, "St Ives". Q was commissioned to complete it. He also started at this time to collect works for his anthology 'The Oxford Book of English Verse.' As he said in a letter to a friend "work tumbles in."

He was also becoming active in politics on behalf of the Liberal Party. Q was opposed to the Boer War and was outspoken in his criticism of British policy. Both of these were unpopular views at the time. In spite of this he was much in demand as a speaker on behalf of the Liberals throughout the country.

It was not all hard work and Q found that he was able to indulge himself in his pleasures with his friends. He had a seven ton cutter, the *Vida*, in which he enjoyed sailing, but he was very fond of rowing. He had a bright red rowing boat and each weekend he and Louisa would visit Atky for a meal at his house at Mixtow, Q rowing there in the daylight and back in the dark. He was very fond of long walks and also horse riding on Crinnis Beach in St Austell Bay.

Life at the club settled into a routine of monthly committee meetings, bar matters, billiards, social contact and sailing. A sailing committee was elected to arrange the August regatta and the 'At home.'

New licensing laws were brought in 1903 and it suddenly came to light during morning golf at the Carlyon Bay course that the Fowey Yacht Club was in danger of losing its license to sell alcohol. It had escaped everyone's notice that application regarding registration of the club had to be made. The closing date for application was upon them but the necessary forms were not available in time. There was an emergency meeting of the committee and legal advice was taken and the crisis averted.

The subject of Royal patronage

Edward the VII was born in 1841. He was Duke of Cornwall and Prince of Wales for a very long time before his accession to the throne in 1902, he had plenty of time to indulge in one of his interests which was sailing.

The Royal Cornwall Yacht Club was founded in Falmouth in 1872. The Mayor of Falmouth was a keen yachtsman and begged the Duke of Cornwall to become patron of the proposed club. He agreed and the club has been known as the Royal Cornwall Yacht Club since its inception.

By 1872 there were fifteen yacht clubs under royal patronage. The first had been the Royal Thames Yacht Club and this was followed by the Royal Yacht Squadron, Cowes.

The designation Royal greatly enhanced the standing of any club. The Fowey Yacht Club management committee was eager for Royal status.

During the time that he was secretary of the club probably around 1898, Q wrote to the Prince of Wales inviting him to accept Honorary Membership of the club. A letter came from Marlborough House, Pall Mall from Francis Knollys who was private secretary to the Prince. In it he expressed the regret of the Prince of Wales, saying, "he is unable to accept the pleasure of complying with your request that he could become an Honorary Member of the Fowey Yacht Club. His Royal Highness wishes it all success but it is contrary to his practice to allow his name to appear in connection with any undertaking which has only recently started and which cannot therefore be regarded as firmly established."

Perhaps Q had not been bold enough. Perhaps he should have begged for patronage like the Royal Cornwall Yacht Club instead of offering Honorary Membership to such an august person.

By 1900 the Prince of Wales had accepted an invitation to become patron of the Royal Western Yacht Club in Plymouth where the Earl of Mount Edgcumbe was Commodore. The following year it was suggested that the Earl of Mount Edgcumbe be written to in order to get the Fowey Club accepted as a Royal Club. This came to nothing.

It was hoped that the Cornish Arms could be included on the club insignia.

However it was discovered that this could only be granted by the Duke of Cornwall and by this time he was out of the country.

At the AGM in the autumn of 1901 it was proposed that the Earl of Mount Edgcumbe be invited to become Commodore of the Fowey Yacht Club in the place of Atky, who had held this office since 1894. This did not find favour with the meeting. The proposer had in fact been a committee member who had been summoned to an extraordinary meeting and fined for after hours drinking with his friend. He had objected to the imposition but finally paid his friend's fine of two shillings and sixpence. He was perhaps unpopular with the committee and his strategy in pursuit of Royal status was rejected.

The impasse was relieved when Captain Edward Treffry suggested that the Earl of Mount Edgcumbe be invited to become Admiral of the Club. Atky was then re-elected Commodore but the question of Royal patronage seems to have been abandoned at this stage.

However, on July 20, 1903 there is a letter written to Q from E Digby, the Home Office, Whitehall:

"Dear Sir,

With reference to your note to Sir G Lushington on the subject of the application to the Fowey Yacht Club for permission to use the style "Royal", I can only say that the application was very carefully considered, in connection with the precedents in similar cases, before the application was refused. The privilege of using the title Royal is only conferred by His Majesty when special claims exist for the grant."

Regretfully the matter was set aside for the time being.

It was on 29 August 1905 that Edward, Prince of Wales, authorised the Fowey Yacht Club to bear on its burgee the insignia of the Duchy Arms surmounted by the Coronet of the Duke of Cornwall. At the same time the Club was informed that the Admiralty was issuing a warrant for a defaced Red Ensign.

This authority given by the Prince of Wales in 1905 was amplified in a letter date 14 November 1952 from Garter King of Arms at the College of Arms. His opinion at that date was that the correct device to be shown on our badge and our Ensign was the Coronet (demi crown) of the eldest son of the Sovereign ie, the coronet (Crown of the Prince of Wales).

Once more in 1905 application was made for the Club to become Royal. It was not until 10th May 1907 that this request was finally granted.

It must have been a matter of great satisfaction to all that the club reputation should be so greatly enhanced in this way. A letter arrived from the home office informing the management committee that his Majesty had authorised the prefix of Royal and "that henceforth the club shall be known as the Royal Fowey Yacht Club".

It was with much pleasure that the secretary ordered new supplies of club stationery bearing the new prefix ROYAL at last.

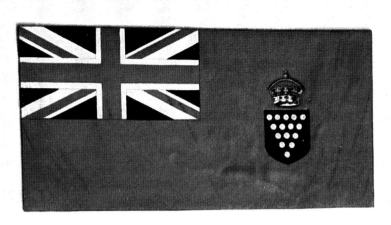

Received from
Somerset Herald & Register
Heralds College.
London.
E.C.

25th October 1905

and on 14th November 1952

Received from

Coronet
of the
Prince of Wales

Rouge Croix
College of Arms
Queen Victoria St.
London E.C4.

ROYAL FOWEY YACHT CLUB

On 25 August 1905 Edward, Prince of Wales authorised the Club burgee bearing the Duchy
Arms surmounted by the Coronet of the Duke of Cornwall.

April 12 1904. The Royal Yacht Victoria and Albert on which HRH Princess Victoria was enjoying a pleasure cruise along the south west coast. The vessel was escorted by Trinity pilots past the town and moored between Place Point and the Bodinnick Ferry. Townspeople thronged every vantage point. At 2.45pm the princess with a party of six gentlemen landed with their bicycles and rode towards Lostwithiel returning at 6pm. Mr Rashleigh of Menabilly sent some lovely flowers from his garden. This picture shows the Royal Yacht leaving Fowey to continue the cruise westward.

Commander Chapman and the ward room officers of H.M. Yacht Victoria and Albert gladly accepted the invitation of the flag officers and members of the Fowey Yacht Club to use their club during the visit of The Royal Yacht to Fowey.

The 1903 Regatta

The Western Morning News reports the 1903 regatta:
"The stormy weather which prevailed on Monday was not promising for the success of the Fowey yacht club Regatta which numbers amongst the most picturesque and enjoyable of yacht fixtures on the Cornish Coast. Yesterday morning the elements were more encouraging, a "jumpy" sea outside the harbour being the only indication of the previous days bad weather. Quite a large number of yachts were unable to reach the port in time for the event. There was a gallant display of bunting in the harbour, the majority of the yachts dressing rainbow fashion. There were about thirty yachts at anchor. In the early part of the afternoon ominous looking clouds made their appearance and occasional heavy showers made matters very uncomfortable for the spectators.

"The bad weather had a detrimental effect on the "at Home" held at the charming premises of the yacht club. A portion of the band of the Royal Marines submitted a charming programme of music.

"Mr H S Tuke's cutter *Flamingo* secured the Vice Commodore's cup beating four other yachts".

Fowey Royal Regatta. The Committee Ship prior to 1905 as there is no coronet above the bezant shield. Notice the smoke from the start cannon and the canopy protecting the many guests on deck.

Henry Scott Tuke was a popular painter who lived and worked in Falmouth. He converted an old French brigantine into a floating studio and was famous for his paintings of shipping and bathers. His close friend was the public benefactor Alfred de Passe. Tuke taught de Passe to sail and soon the pair were locked in sailing rivalry.

Whenever Henry Scott Tuke was not painting he was sailing. He commissioned several boats from Jacketts yard *Red Heart* and *Firefly* and *Flamingo* in which he had many successes. Johnny Jackett the boat builder's son was artists model and boatman for Tuke.

One of the first outings in *Flamingo* was in the summer of 1903 when Tuke, Alfred de Passe and Johnny Jackett sailed to Fowey. He wrote in his diary in June:

"a fair wind but rather rolly passage, carried the topsail for the first time. Strolled around Fowey and dined off cold chicken on board with strawberries. All slept on hard planks"

Alfred de Passe commissioned T Jackett to build him an eighteen foot racing yacht. It was called *Myrtle* after his small daughter. Myrtle was the most serious rival to Jackett's own 18 footer called *Marion*.

In the 1903 regatta the two boats were entered for a race over a course of 12 miles. *Marion* came third to *Myrtle*'s first. The year before the race had been won by *Marion*. Although de Passe had entered *Myrtle* she did not start.

The 1903 win must have given much satisfaction to de Passe. However he soon tired of yachting. Perhaps the weather and discomfort contributed but at the end of the 1903 sailing season he wrote:

"Won several races with the *Myrtle* this year, but disgusted with racing as there was too much feeling and people are always ready to suspect one of cheating, or do it themselves. Resolved not to race next year".

However it is interesting to note that there were no protests during the 1903 regatta at Fowey. All the wins were clear cut and decisive. At the beginning of September there were five new members up for election to the club. One of them was Alfred de Passe, proposed by Arthur Quiller-Couch. In spite of his initial enthusiasm to join the Fowey Yacht Club, Alfred de Passe soon changed his mind. Q reported to the committee that he no longer wished to become a member and his election was annulled.

On board the Committee Ship. Regatta 1913.

Mr Herbert Dampier Phelps, a bachelor who retired from the navy to live in Fowey. A keen yachtsman, he was an early Hon. Sec. of F.Y.C. and close friend of Q.

"And there were roundabouts on the town quay."

Mr Woodcock, Mr Garner, Q, Mr Phelps, Mr Taylor with telescope. Note the "yachting dress" and Q's elegant white boots and striped trousers.

The question of Ladies in the Yacht Club

The Royal Fowey Yacht Club became popular and illustrious men from far afield applied to become members. Membership was confined to men only.

Once a year on club Regatta Day an 'at Home' was held which became a notable occasion in Cornwall and the yachting world. Many famous people and the cream of Cornish society were entertained at the club. Policemen at the two entrances checked invitations and prevented unwelcome visitors from entry.

It was the only time of year when ladies were welcomed to the club.

The women guests wore elegant clothes and lovely hats whilst the men sported white topped caps and all the while a military band stationed by the flagstaff played popular music of the day.

A delicious tea was provided for the guests by the club. Often as many as 250 attended. Catering for them was a considerable undertaking and in the early days Mrs Purcell was responsible for organising this. Later, Foy Quiller-Couch took over the 'at home' teas responsibility. Notes in Foy's own handwriting provide an insight into the complexity of the arrangements: "Treleaven and Miss Rigby (if you care to get cakes from her) like to have their orders early. Suggest not later than the third week in August.

Her detailed account of 'at home' tea preparations continues:

"**China**: all the china comes from Hawkes. They should send it to the club on the Monday morning to give you time to dust it and count it in the afternoon. We supplemented it with extra sugar basins, bread and butter plates and some silver teapots. Julian covers the billiard table with boards. He should do it on Monday morning early. Then newspapers were put on before the cloth went down.

Flowers: The flowers were always provided by Carnethick and arranged by them in their own vases on the Tuesday morning. Roughly it took one large bowl in the centre and four vases for the corners and six glass vases for the tables outside.

Table cloths: The large one for the billiard table belongs to the yacht club. The others for the inside tables were lent. For the outside tables they were borrowed from Fowey Sunday School.

Washing up and drying cloths we can provide.

Coffee: Mother had it made and sent down to the yacht club in big kettles at 3.15pm.

Mr Edward Lewarne, Lostwithiel Street has always done the fire, made the tea and been responsible for getting the tables and chairs to and fro.

Chairs: From the Town Hall.

Chairs: From the Institute.

Muslin bags: Lewarne likes to have one dozen for making the tea in urns.

Ices: Sometimes Lewarne has served these and sometimes Treleaven.

Removal of windows: This was done easily on the Tuesday morning and put back by him on Tuesday night.

Band.

Awnings.

Trays: About six are wanted, mainly for the ices.

Helpers: About four of us went down on the Monday afternoon or evening to dust and count the china and again on the Tuesday morning to unpack and arrange the cakes.

Paid helpers: Mrs Philp of Newtown came at 10.30am and cut up sandwiches, bread and butter and splits until 3.30pm. Then she stayed on and washed up after. She was paid five shillings.

The others: Ten in number came at 10.30am and cut up sandwiches, bread and butter and splits until 3.30pm then they stayed on and washed up after and were paid 2/6 each.

Three pour inside at three square tables placed by the windows. The tables are collected from various rooms and have green baize tops.

One hands around and refills plates.

One runs for and back from the window to the washing up tub.

Five are in charge of outside tables. After the tea ices are served on the outside tables. After it is over anything that is cut up is divided by you between the helpers.

If possible count the china and the spoons the same evening."

Perhaps these notes were written in 1933 when Mrs de Cressey Treffry agreed to help with the 'at home.' They provide vivid insight into the amount of organisation needed 'behind the scenes' to make the Regatta 'at home' a success.

The bar was an important facility in the club and a considerable stock was carried. By July 1902 because there was insufficient storage space it was discussed that an outhouse should be built at the back of the club. However, Mrs Mills offered the use of a cave in the cliff wall at the back of the premises at a rent of five shillings per annum. Later it was agreed to erect an awning over the entrance. This was made by a sailmaker in the town and protected the Steward from rain. These days the entrance to the cave is blocked.

Ever since the early days of the club there has been a wide range of drinks available. In 1897 there was a choice of five champagnes, claret, burgundy, sherry, hock and port.

A variety of liqueurs were available. Green chartreuse and Kummel at 6d a glass and sloe gin at 5d a glass. Sherry and bitters and gin and bitters were on sale at 5d a glass and peach bitters at 4d a glass. Beer was sold at 3d or 4d a bottle, either Bass or Salts Pale Ale and Allsopps Ale was available on draught at 2d a glass.

Cigars were popular. Carvajals Havana cigars were sold at 6d and 4d each. Litsica and Marx cigarettes were sold singly. Vasso at 1d or alternatively Kaliniki. Sweet Caporal cigarettes were sold in packets of ten at 6d a packet. All were supplied by Fowey Wine Co Ltd.

Arthur Quiller-Couch's civic duties

Although he worked hard for the Yacht Club Q's activities were not confined to Fowey. Soon after the formation of the Cornwall County Education Committee he was elected to its membership. For the next 30 years he served either as chairman or vice chairman. During that time he visited over 300 schools on poor roads in 'ramshackle hired conveyances'. The intention was to provide accessible secondary education to every child in Cornwall.

In 1907 Q was appointed Justice of the Peace. He was also actively involved with Liberal election campaigners with his yacht club all Mr Allchin of Tredudwell, a house near Polruan. Mr Allchin was a small man, but a big Liberal. He would wear a large blue and yellow rosette during the run up to the elections. Apparently election time was a lot of fun in Fowey and Polruan. Everyone would go to the meetings which were held in both townships. When the results came in during the afternoon of the day following polling everyone would watch to see what colour flag would be hoisted over Q's house. In 1906 there was a landslide Liberal victory and a new government was formed under the premiership of Asquith.

On July 30, 1910 at the annual summer general meeting of the club the Commodore offered the hearty congratulations of the members of the club to Q on the honour which had recently been conferred to him by the King. In June 1910 Q was knighted by King George V at St James Palace in recognition of his combined services to literature, education and politics. It was a popular knighthood and on his return to Fowey the band of the Volunteers assembled outside the Haven and played 'A Fine Old English Gentleman' and other appropriate airs.

The members were eager to share in the glamour of the occasion. On November 30 the Royal Fowey Yacht Club arranged a dinner in Q's honour. Subscriptions of 10/6 were invited by the Honorary Secretary Norman P Jaffrey. The dinner cost 7/6 per ticket excluding wine. It was held at the St Catherine's Hotel. The Commodore, Edward Atkinson, sat at the head of the table with Q to his right. There were 22 other members dining also when a presentation to Q was made.

By his own efforts Q had made a life for himself that was successful and exciting. As Rear Commodore he continued to work hard to maintain the success that the club had become. However it is not possible to please everyone all of the time as the following criticisms in the Suggestions Book show.

September 18, 1906
"I suggest that a Bible be placed among the books in the reading room. I was anxious to find a quotation from scripture for a member today but on inquiring found that apparently there is not a copy of the sacred book on the premises."
H N Purcell, Vicar.

November 17, 1908

"May I suggest that a light be placed outside the club entrance? On dark nights one is easily liable to strike either the post supporting the awning or else the wooden shrub tubs. This is especially the case when there is no light in the billiard or card room."

J E Justin.

1914

"Can nothing be done to mitigate the nuisance caused by cows at the main entrance to the club? For the past two days the entrance has been almost impassable owing to the filth upon the footpath. Surely the owner of the cows could be made to remove any deposits upon the footpaths."

J E Justin

Cows which grazed in the fields on the edge of the town were herded each day down Lostwithiel Street to their milking parlour behind the Toll Bar house. Their route included part of the footpath to the yacht club.

★ ★ ★ ★ ★ ★ ★ ★ ★ ★ ★ ★ ★

Q's son Bevil was growing into a handsome teenager. He was golden haired and much admired by his family who called him "The Boy."

Kenneth Grahame's wife Elspeth wrote:

"The eight year old page at our wedding was Bevil Quiller-Couch - a splendid little fellow who even at that age was so clever and so sensible that his opinion was weighted and gravely taken, as later it came to be sought and valued alike by townspeople and sailor men. He grew up to be what he then promised - a tower of strength, ever to be relied on, cheerful and charming with a genius for friendship in every walk of life and for those of all ages."

On September 14, 1909 Bevil had been elected to the club. He was 19 years of age. In April of the following year he was elected to the sailing committee. He entered Trinity College, Oxford in January 1910. During the summer vacation he spent a lot of the time yachting, either with undergraduate friends or with the Commodore Atky for they had become firm friends.

1911 was a busy year for Q. Although the club was now holding monthly dinners at 2/6 per head Q only managed to attend three of them. Bevil accompanied him to the function in April. Together they were making plans for the Coronation.

Mr Herbert Phelps and Mr Jaffrey and friends on the water

H.D. Phelps rowing in a different hat.

In 1892 Gottleib Daimler and William Steinway, the German piano manufacturer devised a petrol outboard engine for boats. By 1914 they were everywhere. Arthur Quiller-Couch never had one., he preferred to row himself about the harbour. Here we see Q's R.Y.C. associate Mr Jaffrey and his companion. It is thought that the outboard engine is a Swan.

Another way of crossing the river was at the Bodinnick Ferry. This picture shows the horse ferry. One man steadies the pony whilst the others row with long oars called sweeps.

Bevil's yacht Swastika moored at Helford.

The Coronation of King George V, 1911

The coronation of King George V took place on June 2, 1911 and once again Q found time from his other activities to help prepare the town's celebrations. He was familiar with such events, having organised civic celebrations throughout his time in Fowey. This time there were two military bands, evergreen arches, a military gun salute from the Town Quay, houses and boats decorated with coloured lights and a fancy dress ball to be arranged in the Armoury. But this time there was a pageant too, enacted in the grounds of Place. It was written by Q and entitled 'This Royal Throne of Kings.' Q was aided in this production by Bevil, now 20 years old. In spite of all the demands on his time, Q did not neglect the yacht club. He attended most of the committee meetings to plan the regatta events later on in the summer.

Regatta day was Tuesday August 15. The Royal Cruising Club had arranged to visit Fowey during their summer cruise. They were made honorary members of the club for the duration of regatta week and entertained to a dinner in the Drill Hall the day after the regatta. An almost total absence of wind robbed the day of excitement. Races were long drawn out affairs. Courses were shortened and the races turned into tedious drifting matches. Several boats abandoned the competition and rowed home with the aid of sweeps (long oars). Only two boats competed for the Commodore's Cup and took nearly seven hours to sail 18 miles. The Vice Commodore's Cup was won by Mr S B Harbey's *Florence* after racing for more than nine hours.

Mrs Purcell had agreed to undertake the management of the 'at home' on the terrace. There was an unusually large attendance so it was fortunate that the day was one of brilliant sunshine. Music was supplied during the afternoon by the band of the Plymouth Division of the RMLI under Band Sergeant Pike.

A few days later at the summer AGM, Atky was re-elected Commodore and Q was re-elected Rear Commodore. Mr C P Johnson resigned from the post of Vice Commodore after many years of valuable service and Mr R Davey was elected in his place. The heatwave persisted into September. The Western Morning News wrote:

"The continued heat this summer has never been surpassed since official records have been taken, over a period of seventy years. The temperature has hovered around 80 degrees. Little did those think who felt the atmosphere cooling and heard the wind rising on Saturday night that the break in the summer of 1911 was to be signalled by such a catastrophe as this."

But catastrophe was imminent.

Summer's end

The Quiller-Couchs always dined at 7.30pm, often with friends. Bevil was home from Oxford for the summer vacation so it is probable that at the dinner party on Saturday September 9 he and Atky discussed their plan for a moonlight sail. At about 10pm they left the harbour in an 18ft sailing boat, *The Gymnotis* owned by Atky. Their intention was to sail to Looe. The weather forecast for the day had indicated light to moderate northerly winds. The temperature was falling and thundery showers were expected but in Fowey at 10.30pm it was a delightful moonlit night. However, once they left the harbour the wind picked up and blew from the east. The pair decided that it was unwise to carry on so they anchored in the lee of Pencarrow head at about midnight. By 6am next morning they set off for Fowey as the wind had gone around to the south-east and had abated a little.

The boat was an interesting one. Although classed as a canoe it probably resembled a Clyde Canoe Club One Design, which was in reality a small centreboard yacht. The boat was fitted with fore and aft watertight air tanks which they thought were copper lined. The boat was meant to be unsinkable and the friends were confident of this in spite of the rough conditions. They had set out across Lantic Bay with the sails reefed when a strong gust of wind hit them "over the helm and struck her on the beam." The well of the boat filled with water and they began to bale. Then the boat dipped in the stern and they realised that the aft air tank was leaking and the boat was sinking under them. It was drifting to leeward and rougher water so they had no choice but to make for the shore about 500 yards away. Atky, white faced and semi-conscious and supported by an air cushion was towed to the rocks by Bevil. As they approached the shore the boat sank out of sight. Bevil was unable to help his friend onto the steep rocks on the shore. The heavy swell was breaking and washing them back, making it impossible for the exhausted Atky to leave the water. After several attempts he signalled Bevil to go ashore.

The cliffs around Lantic Bay are high and steep and there is no easy way up to the fields; it is an exhausting climb. The nearest farm is that at Churchtown, Lanteglos, half a mile away and it was here that Bevil finally managed to raise the alarm. The farmer's son, E Barnicoat, galloped on horseback to the Polruan Coastguards, who called the pilots. The tug was called and a search began, but nothing was found. Atky had disappeared.

All day Sunday and Monday search parties looked for his body. Q and his boatman Edward Grose in one boat; Charles Hanson and his boatman in another, and Bevil in another. Finally Charles Hunkin and his son George and four men guided their boat to a gully where the water was about five feet deep and it was there that they found him. They dragged his body into the boat and a motor launch towed them back to Fowey. They laid his body in his own boathouse at Mixtow. His pocket watch had stopped at 6am.

All of Fowey was stunned. Atky was a man who was widely known and greatly respected. On Sunday evening in Fowey Church Canon Purcell paid tribute to his friend: "Pleasant, kindly, helpful, I do not believe he was ever appealed to in vain. His hand was an ever open one to relieve the distressed. Many will mourn for him. Many will also miss him."

At the yacht club the Vice Commodore Mr R Davey referred to the great loss the club had sustained. It was proposed that Canon Purcell be asked to write and convey to Miss Marston and the late Commodore's friends the sympathy of the officers and members. It was also agreed that an appreciation of Mr Bevil Quiller-Couch's splendid efforts and conduct throughout be recorded in the minutes. Arrangements for the club to be represented at the funeral were left in the hands of the Rear Commodore. Before the funeral though there had to be an inquest.

This was held in the sitting room at Mixtow House, the home of Miss Marston, Atky's cousin and housekeeper. There was just enough room for the jury and officials and only three witnesses were called. Mr A de Castro Glubb, the County Coroner for the district conducted the enquiry. Mr F A Allchin, an old friend of Q's was the foreman of the jury. Q was called to identify the deceased. Bevil was summoned next. "I live in Fowey and am a friend of the deceased." He was questioned by the coroner.

Q: When was it you went on this little boating expedition?

A: On Saturday last, the 9th inst.

Q: You and the deceased left about what time?

A: About 10.30pm. The intention was to go to Looe if the wind served, but the chief object was to have a sail by moonlight and return in the morning.

Q: What sort of boat was it?

A: A sailing canoe.

Q: How big was it, and did it carry a mast?

A: It was 16 feet in length I think. A mast and two sails.

Q: What tonnage would she be?

A: About one and a half I should think.

Q: I suppose you rowed out.

A: No, we sailed out.

Q: Was the boat protected by any air chambers or what?

A: She had two bulkheads which were supposed to be airtight.

Q: One at each end.

A: Yes.

Q: She was supposed to be unsinkable.

A: Yes.

Q: Was she an old boat or a new one?

A: It was a fairly old boat, but she was kept in good condition.

Q: Would she be stored under cover?

A: Undercover in winter but moored off the Quay in the open in summer.

Q: Then it has been moored in the open for some considerable period?

A: Yes.

Q: All the summer in fact.

A: As far as I know.

Q: Wouldn't a boat get cracked a bit in such circumstances?

A: Not if she is well varnished.

Q: Tell us what happened.

A: We sailed out of the harbour towards Looe. We started out just as the wind came down from the east. We made one tack of a mile and a half and on coming back decided as soon as we got under the lee of Pencarrow Head that we had better anchor. We got there at midnight and stopped there until about six in the morning, when we started for Fowey, two and a half miles away. The wind was about south east and had gone down somewhat. It had been exceeding strong in the night. We took in one reef. A strong puff came down over the helm and struck her hard on the beam.

Q: Did the boat capsize?

A: No - the well of the boat filled and almost immediately the after bulkhead filled with water. The boat then dipped at the stern.

Q: Did she go right under?

A: Not at first. We pulled the mainsail down and I heard the air rushing out of the bow bulkhead, and knew it was only a question of time. Then I talked to the deceased and we decided it was best to leave the boat at once as she was drifting to leeward, where the sea was rougher. We were about four hundred yards from the shore. The deceased could swim but he had his clothes on while I ripped off all but my shirt. There were two or three airtight cushions including one double one across which I laid him. He was not strong and shocked to find the boat going down. He moved his hands a bit and I pulled him. I was swimming with my legs and chiefly on my back. We got to the shore.

Q: What sort of shore was it?

A: Steep rocks clean out of the water and no beach. It was high tide. We discussed what to do and the chances of getting round to the beach, but we were against the wind.

Q: He was exhausted by this time, but sensible and able to talk to you?

A: He was very white and exhausted. We made for the rocks and got within ten yards of the shore when we met the rebound of the waves and I couldn't pull him in. We tried to land at one place and then went a little to the east. I landed for a minute or two and then went out again, but he motioned me to go ashore and get help. I shouted to him but I don't think he heard. I climbed the rocks.

Q: As long as he had strength enough to keep on the cushion he would have been alright?

A: Yes.

Q: You got help?

A: Yes. I went up over some field to Churchtown Farm and met Mr Barnicoat the farmer in the orchard. It was about half past six or seven. He called his son and sent him to Polruan. I got some clothes and cycled after him.

Q: Couldn't you get ropes?

A: Not long ones, and I thought the other way was quicker. I intended going in the boat but I met the Coastguard and the pilot and they stopped a tug that belonged to the harbour and went out in her. I did not go out but went back to the cliff. I saw the cushion float around the point.

Q: Then you knew he was dead.

A: Oh yes. The place is called Lantic Bay and is in Lanteglos Parish.

Q: Why do you think these two bulkheads gave way? Did the wood break in?

A: Oh no. The stern chamber filled at once. I think the wood got cracked while the boat had been lying in the harbour during the summer.

William Charles Hunkin, a boatman of Fowey said he found the body on Monday in Lantic Bay. It was in the water. "We got it into the boat" said the witness "and brought it here to Mixtow."

The coroner concluded:

"That is all the evidence necessary gentlemen to enable you to arrive at your verdict. It is a very dreadful tragedy that has happened and I am sure everyone cannot help saying young Mr Quiller-Couch did everything that could possibly be done to save his companion (Hear Hear)."

The jury returned a verdict of accidental drowning and the foreman added: "The jury wishes to express their sincere sympathy in this loss with the family and to express their high appreciation of the conduct of Mr Quiller-Couch.

The funeral took place the next day. At 10am about 30 boats and motor launches assembled at the quay at Mixtow. The coffin, covered with wreaths of flowers was brought down from the house and placed on a boat which was towed by a motor launch with its flag at half mast. Other launches fell into line, each towing two or three boats. Many other boats joined the procession as it turned into Pont Creek. At the top of the creek bearers carried the coffin up the steep path to the church at Lanteglos. There the procession was met by the vicar, the Reverend C F Trusted and Atky's old club friend Canon Purcell.

Sixteen yachtsmen took it in turns to be bearers all wearing guernseys with bright red lettering. The bearer party acted under instruction of Herbert Dampier Phelps. The choir was made up of boys from the Fowey Grammar School where Atky had been a governor for many years, and boys from Fowey Church Choir.

There were many mourners. Amongst the lovely wreaths there was a tribute from the Fowey Yacht Club - the Commodore's flag of scarlet and yellow dahlias with a raised crown and the county arms on a black plush shield.

At the graveside the choir sang unaccompanied the verse of the hymn 'Our life is but a fading dawn.'

By LOUIS PAUL.

FIT FOR NORTH SEA GALES

A handy little local cruiser

Florence winning Channel Race Plymouth

Cynthia - first in Channel Race from Falmouth

Q elected Commodore

Now that Atky was gone, life at the yacht club must have been subdued. Bevil was able to get away from the gloom, returning to the excitement of student life at Oxford. For those left behind it was the sad time of year for yachtsmen when their craft are laid up for winter. At the AGM of the club on November 22, 1911 it was reported that membership of the club was now 226 and the yacht tonnage 4,564. It was recorded what a deep loss the club had sustained by the death of the Commodore.

It was unanimously resolved to elect Q the new Commodore of the club. It is curious that the Vice Commodore Mr R Davey did not become Commodore. Perhaps he was ill for he died two months later on January 9, 1912. Mr G T Petherick was elected Rear Commodore and Mr Justice Channel was elected Vice Commodore.

Kenneth Grahame visited Fowey once more in the autumn of 1911. He wrote to his American friend Austin Purves: "I loved Atky - perhaps in a selfish way, first of all because his special "passions" appealed to me - boats, Bohemianism, Burgundy, tramps, travel, books and pictures - but also and I hope and believe chiefly for his serene and gentle nature, his unfailing good humour and his big, kind heart. Again and again, in imagination, I get my boat at Whitehouse steps and scull up the river by the grey old sea wall, under the screaming gulls past the tall Russian and Norwegian ships at their moorings and so into Mixtow Pill, and ship my oars at the little stone pier and find Atky waiting on the steps, thin, in blue serge, with his Elizabethan head: and stroll up the pathway you know to the little house above it, and he talking all the time and always some fresh whimsicality. I had a letter a very few weeks ago telling of a Yachting Dinner they had just had, he apparently in the chair and his spirits seemed as buoyant as ever."

Later, Kenneth Grahame and his wife visited the house at Mixtow which was now for sale. They toyed with the idea of buying it themselves, but as he wrote to Purves: "it's not to be let, and I don't think it will sell in a hurry - it is not everybody's house." Abandoned and neglected Atky's collections of objets d'art, paintings and tin toys were rapidly deteriorating to become a houseful of old junk. The place was damp and cold and the magic had gone.

* * * * * * * * * * * * *

In the yacht club the pattern of activities continued much as before. Although nine members had died in 1912 by the time of the AGM the membership had increased once more to a total of 238. Yacht tonnage was 4,300. It was decided that the dues for temporary membership of the club should be one shilling per day or one guinea for a month and that the steward should have a striped jacket for morning wear.

Mrs Purcell agreed to organise the 'at home' which was by now quite a large undertaking.

In 1913 membership had again risen, this time to 244 although the yacht tonnage had fallen to 4,025. At the AGM on November 26, 1913 the treasurer revealed that the regatta had run at a deficit. Eight members including Q agreed to underwrite it.

Q writes in October 1913: "This ritual of laying up the boat is our way of bidding farewell to the summer. It is on a slackening flood tide that we cast off our moorings and head up the river with our backs to the waning sunset. Since we tow a dinghy astern and are ourselves towed by the silent boatman you could call it a procession. She has been stripped during the last two days of sails, rigging and all spars but the main mast. Now we bring her alongside the town quay and the mast creaks as it is lifted out of its step. We lower it, lay it along the deck and resume our way, past quay doors and windows where already the town folk are beginning to light their lamps and so by the jetties where foreign crews rest with their elbows on bulwarks and stare down upon us, idly through the dusk. She is only a little cutter of six tons, but what memories we lay up with the boat.

So we near the beach where she is to lie. Astern the jettymen and stevedores are wrangling, trains are shunting, cranes working, trucks discharging their cargoes amid clouds of dust. The boatman rests on his oars, the tow rope slackens. She glides into the deep shadow of the shore and with a soft grating noise takes ground. Silently we carry her chain out and noose it about a monster elm. Silently we slip legs under her channels, lift and make fast her stern moorings, lash the tiller for the last time and tie coverings over the cabin top. An hour perhaps passes, and November darkness has settled on the river before we push off our boat, committing her to winter. As we thread our dim way homeward among the riding lights flickering on the black water the last pale vision of her, alone and lightless, follows me and reminds me of the dull winter ahead, the short days and long nights.

I land on the wet slip strewn with dead leaves at the tide's edge and walk up the hill home. I open my library door and lo, a bright fire burning and smiling and over against the blaze of it cheerful companionable, my books have been awaiting me".

On October 31, 1912 Q was appointed King Edward VII Professor of English Literature at Cambridge, and by November was in Cambridge on duty and also house-hunting. The plan was that Lady Quiller-Couch and "the babe", their daughter Foy, should stay with Q during term time and return to their home during the vacations. Bevil was continuing his studies at Oxford. The servants from the Haven were to accompany the family. The household was established at a rented house in Cambridge by the autumn of 1913. Q attended very few Fowey yacht club committee meetings in 1913. On August 4, 1914 war was declared on Germany and the Quiller-Couches were back in residence at the Haven, all except for Bevil. He had joined the Officers Training Corps when he went up to Oxford and had transferred to the Special Reserve in 1913. In August 1914 he was immediately called up for service as a second lieutenant in the Royal Field Artillery. By the end of August he was in France with the British Expeditionary Force.

THE YACHTING MONTHLY. 373

The "De Wets" overhang is much appreciated by a Fowey gallant!

The Loch Etive — another fine old Australian clipper for the scrap heap.

The 12 metre CYRA slips out past the old castle —

WORK AND PLAY — the Rotterdam steamer on her way out —

The Great War, 1914-18

The Great War totally disrupted the routine of ordinary life. At a meeting of the yacht club committee on August 8, 1914 it was resolved to abandon the regatta and return the subscriptions that had already been paid.

Trench warfare in France began on September 16 that year and by the time of the AGM on November 25, about 50 yacht club members were serving in His Majesty's Forces. It was announced with deep regret the loss to the club of Lieutenant R C Graves Sawle who had been killed in action. Two other members were reported to be wounded and detained as prisoners of war. There was a sharp decline in profit from wine and spirits accounts.

Q had been a leading member of the Territorial Force Association in Cornwall ever since it was formed in 1908. When war was declared he was at once involved in recruiting campaigns, forming new units as quickly as possible. He was allowed time away from his duties at Cambridge to allow his recruitment work. When he did return to his university work Lady Quiller-Couch stayed in Fowey and Q lived in rooms at Jesus College. Whenever they were separated Q would write daily letters to his wife and did so for the rest of his life. This led to a great accumulation of letters which Lady Quiller-Couch destroyed after his death.

With the onset of war all pleasure yachting stopped. Access to the water was banned and blocked and stepladders were removed. The club dinghy was rendered unusable and barbed wire appeared on the rails of the club terrace.

On December 8, 1914 there was a club meeting where it was decided that the Commodore and flag officers should invite the Colonel and officers of the 12th Worcestershire Regiment, stationed in Fowey, to become honorary members of the club.

As more units were stationed in the area there were more such invitations which included the Colonel and officers of the 2nd Seventh Devons. The club by now had changed to a social, drinking and billiard club for young officers who were in training prior to their embarkation to France.

In February 1915 it was reported that 16 club members on active service had not paid their dues and it was resolved that no action be taken. In June 1915 the 12th Battalion of the Worcester Regiment presented the club with a gift before they left Fowey for France.

There was another gift in July. Four years after the death of her cousin Atky, Miss Marston presented to the club the model of the figurehead of *Airymouse*. It was this carving that had been made for the bronze casting of the actual figurehead on the boat. For many years this wooden *Airymouse* decorated the billiard room, but it has since disappeared.

Q was not able to attend meetings in 1915 but he was re-elected Commodore in his absence. From March to October 1915 he was on military duty in Cornwall

1914. Troops prepare to leave Fowey for war.

raising a battalion of the Duke of Cornwall's Light Infantry and putting them through their initial training. He was made a temporary lieutenant and then promoted to captain three months later. He worked extremely long hours and in the middle of it all set papers for the final degree exams in Cambridge, but he was late completing them, so badly was he pressed by his military work.

Q's own battalion was 210 strong. After a hard morning's drill he describes taking them on a route march in the afternoon. He was considered to be an eccentric leader by his recruits. He insisted on them shaving every day and inspected their chins every morning at 9.30am. The unforgettable eccentricity of this kindly leader was revealed on the day he took his whole company back home for tea after a route march. The day was fine and they sat at tables in the garden of the Haven and Lady Quiller-Couch provided them with teas until "the cupboard was bare." Even more bizarre was the day when the company was encouraged to swim in the sea and Q cut the overlong toenails of soldiers himself. No doubt many had feet made more comfortable by this almost biblical tender care.

By 1916 the Commodore was back in Cambridge lecturing on the Art of Reading. There were many women students at this time but few young men as so many were

Tea party at the Haven for Q's new D.C.L.I. recruits Lady Quiller-Couch in foreground, Foy Quiller-Couch to her left holding jug. Sir Arthur Quiller-Couch standing on right near trellis. The tables are decorated with valerian, Pride of Fowey, Q's favourite flowers.

away on national service. Q found life very hard and lived in constant anxiety for his son Bevil who was engaged in heavy fighting in France.

It is not surprising that there were many yacht club meetings that Q was unable to attend and various committee members deputised for the Commodore and chaired meetings. But he was back in Fowey for Christmas. He wrote from the Haven afterwards:

"I cheer up because my Boy has been home and imparted life to the whole situation. They have made him a major." He continued: "I am writing lectures for next term and am simply boiling over with plots of plays and novels and schemes of books etc and I have this day sawn up about three hundredweight of wood on my own farm, corrected about one third of that weight of proofs and dined sparsely but as a Christian. The carollers have been singing in the hall and holly and ivy make the usual background. Also it has been a heavenly December day. At 12.30am a British airship came swooping low over the house."

Throughout 1916 the club continued to confer many honorary memberships. Losses continued, both natural ones and those caused by death in active service. Membership dropped to 214 and there was no indication of tonnage because of the war. By March 1917 it was decided to increase the wine and spirit charges. A whisky and soda now cost 8d and a Guinness stout 5d. It was also agreed that "stimulants" should only be sold to members at such hours as are permitted by law. There were now many honorary members from Fowey Convalescent Hospital. these were wounded young men recuperating at Fowey before returning to the front. Colonel Earle was the Commanding Officer of the Convalescent Hospital. He requested that no "stimulants" should be supplied to convalescent officers except during meals.

Q was re-elected Commodore of the club at the AGM in August 1917. The membership of the club remained much the same as the previous year at 213, but there were many more temporary members using the facilities. The billiard table needed recovering and a ventilator was installed in the lavatory. There were many complaints of bad odours. The facilities were not designed for such heavy use.

More deaths were reported including that of the Earl of Mount Edgcumbe. As temporary members left Fowey to fight in France there was a great accumulation of abandoned property in the club. Canon Purcell suggested that arrangements be made to store raincoats and oilers which were hanging on the pegs in the hall and causing an obstruction. The steward was instructed to remove them to the bathroom where they could be stored until reclaimed. It is a sad fact that many young men did not survive and never returned to claim their lost garments.

There were obviously money problems. The steward was instructed not to cash any cheques for temporary members or honorary members. Permanent members were still to have this privilege. Early in 1917 it became apparent that there was consistent loss of profits on gin, port and brandy. Examination of finances revealed errors of accounting on the balance sheets on two occasions, each time in favour of the steward. In April he resigned. The next steward was appointed at a salary of £52 per annum with rooms, coal and gas expenses included but by May of the following year there was yet another change of steward.

At the 1918 AGM Q was again elected Commodore, Sir Arthur Channel was elected Vice Commodore and Mr G T Petherick was elected Rear Commodore.

Problems with the lavatory had persisted and the notice over the urinal had been defaced. The Honorary Secretary was instructed to make enquiries among the members as to who had done this. He was also instructed to call the matter to the attention of Colonel Lloyd Williams, C O of the Fowey Convalescent Hospital to the matter. It seems that Colonel Lloyd Williams responded by thanking the club for the hospitality extended to the patients of the Convalescent Hospital. There were even more officers recovering from their wounds who were housed in various hotels in the town before returning to France after recovery. These hotels included the Fowey Hotel and St Catherine's Hotel.

It seemed as if the war would go on for ever at the beginning of 1918. Bravely Q continued with his duties in Cambridge but he was more able to cope back home in Fowey. During the summer months he organised teams of boys and girls to help with the harvest in the fields around the town.

September was a joyous time for the whole family, for Bevil was again home on leave. Q wrote in a letter:

"We've had a heavenly time. It wound up with our sailing him up the river here, seven miles to Lostwithiel Station and seeing him and his sister off to a two day riot of shopping and theatre going. Then his mother and I pulled home on the ebb on the dusk of a lovely evening, but it was very much on the ebb and very much in the dusk. Mothers are wonderful."

The war ended on November 11. Q described later how the news reached him in Cambridge:

"A jolly man rushing into a shop shouted to the woman shopkeeper that the guns had ceased fire and she could stop fretting about her man." He continued "The awful strain was over at last and to one who for four years had endured it was not only the salvation of his country achieved, there was also release from the awful dragging anxiety of his own, the hideous terror of any telegraph boy walking towards his house. For those of us loving our sons the strain had been too long."

There was a yacht club AGM on November 26, 1918. There had been 529 honorary memberships granted to convalescent officers and others during the four years of the war. There had been 214 deaths of members in the past five years.

Sir Arthur Quiller-Couch took most of his guests to visit the land he had cultivated behind Prime Cellars on the east bank of the river. Q called it "The Farm". This picture shows a family picnic, probably 1915. Lady Quiller-Couch is seated between her daughter Foy and Q's great friend and yacht club colleague Herbert Dampier Phelps. Bevil's dog, Jory, is at their feet.

Bevil

Bevil Bryan Quiller-Couch was idolised by his family. He was the first born child in 1890 when his father was still working in London. Bevil was named after Q's civil war hero Sir Bevil Grenville, but he was known by other names within the family, "Piper" and "Pippa" when he was very small and the "Boy" or "The Boy" as he grew older. He was a well-known and popular child in Fowey, a fine boy and the apple of his father's eye.

Until he went to preparatory school Bevil lived with his parents in Fowey. As a boy Q had hoped to go to Winchester himself, but the headmaster of his preparatory school had forgotten to send in his application in time. In many ways Q must have hoped that Bevil would enjoy the chances he would have wished for himself and so Bevil was educated at Winchester College.

Before Bevil left home for his preparatory school Q wrote: "The boy is learning Latin with me, is quite clever at it, and I am growing quite keen. I should like to make a pretty scholar of him but he'll go to school and then Lord knows what will happen."

Form III, Horris Hill School. Bevil Quiller-Couch on right at side of window.

His preparatory school was Horris Hill in Devon.

An old school report of Bevil's, found in Fowey, gives some indication of what he managed. The average age of 11 years and 4 months in a class of 13 boys shows Bevil bottom of the class in Classics. The comments were as follows: "At present he knows practically no Latin, but he is doing his best and seems anxious to improve." His prose was no better, where his position was 12th out of 13. "At present he has no idea of writing the simplest sentence down correctly." In mathematics: "Can't do simple sums right but is getting better." It must have been a relief to his parents that his conduct was reported "good."

Although Bevil was no scholar he was an athlete and excelled at rowing like his father. Bevil was a keen yachtsman and often sailed with Atky, the Commodore of the yacht club. As soon as he was old enough he was elected a member of the club and would attend yacht club dinners which were held regularly in the town at St Catherine's Hotel or the Fowey Hotel. He was later elected to the sailing committee of the club.

In January 1910 Bevil went up to Oxford. Q had kept up his friendship with Charles Cannan from his Fleet Street days and in 1908 in November he received a letter from Charles' three daughters. They had compiled a book of poems and Q had contributed one of his own compositions. They thanked him for his contribution and were all looking forward to the publication of their book. They said: "We hope your son will come and stay with us when he comes up for his exams to get into Trinity."

Bevil was a frequent visitor to the Cannan's home in Magdalene Gatehouse, Oxford. It must have given Q great pleasure that a romance developed between Bevil and Charles' second daughter May Wedderburn Cannan. Many couples waited for the war to end before embarking on marriage. So did May and Bevil. They wrote to each other constantly. Whilst Bevil was involved in continuous fighting on the front line May was doing war work in Paris. The Armistice was signed on November 11 and when Bevil returned to Paris he was carried on a chariot draped with flowers and bunting and pulled through the streets with French and Swiss heroes and British Tommies. There was dancing and singing hand in hand, processions and confetti. They had a blissful five days together and Bevil asked May to marry him. They announced their engagement and arranged a date in June for their wedding. Q wrote to May:

> "My very dear Child, it is rather pleasant you know when two young people conspire to fulfil what would have been man's dearest wish. This of course means, among other things, wishing myself joy, after four and a half years of pitching one's hope no higher than that Bevil might have come through it safely."

Bevil's unit was one that was chosen to march into Germany, part of the army of occupation. In January 1919 Bevil was on leave and took May to Fowey. Later May wrote of the visit to the Haven:

*Trinity IV, 2nd sitting, 1910. Bow. C.R. Bury, 10.4; 2. B.B. Quiller-Couch, 11.8;
3. H.F. Graham, 12.4; Str. F. E. Buller, 10.4*

"We helped a little in the orchard garden that they called "The Farm", rowing over in the old Red Boat. We sailed out to sea in *True Tilda* and met a small gale. We walked in Cornish headland and he showed me Menabilly, which he said he would like and Kilmarth which I said I would like because it was smaller. You could see over the lift of a hayfield the dazzle that was his sea. We went to a party where he was surrounded by people who loved him. We dined in the Haven of an evening, and there was silver and wine in tall glasses and candlelight. And then it was over. He was to go back to duty. I said goodbye to him and went back to the quiet drawing room and lamplight and the sound of the sea washing the rocks below the garden wall."

Bevil returned to his unit in Germany. He told his parents that he felt responsible for the men under him, "my children" he called them. He prepared to stay with them until they were all demobilised - and the horses too - and were all able to return to England. Bevil was extremely fond of his own horse, a mare named Peggy, who served with him throughout the war. On his return to Fowey Bevil was to take up a post with a shipping agency at a modest salary of £300 per year. May and Bevil looked forward to the future confident in their shared happiness.

Meanwhile, back in Fowey, people began to pick up the threads of ordinary life again. A meeting of the committee of the Royal Fowey Yacht Club was arranged for January 14. A letter had come from the YRA, the national body which preceded the RYA. The club were notified of a meeting to be held in London to discuss what steps should be taken in order to revive yacht racing generally. The committee resolved to send a representative to that meeting. They also decided to select a sailing committee to organise the resumption of yachting in Fowey. It was agreed to hold a regatta on August 9 with a modified 'at home.'

On a more mundane level it was once again discussed that there were many complaints about the bad smell from the lavatory. It was decided to obtain expert advice at last. Q returned to Cambridge to resume his professional duties and Lady Quiller-Couch and Foy were thankful to stay at home in Fowey and plan for the wedding.

Then on the evening of February 6, 1919 Q received a telegram informing him that Bevil was dangerously ill. By the first available train he returned to his wife in Fowey just before a second telegram arrived informing them that Bevil was dead. He had died of pneumonia after a short illness of just a few days. Probably he was a victim of Spanish Influenza which raged through Europe at that time. After the ravages and depletions of war people's defences against infection were low. The infection was a virulent one and there were many deaths. It was a world wide epidemic which spread to Europe in August and England in October. 150,000 English people died of influenza in the winter of 1918 - 1919. In India there were 16 million deaths.

Q and Bevil's fiancée, May, met in London at once. They hoped to get permission from the War Office to attend Bevil's funeral, but it was not forthcoming. There was a difficulty with passports and they were unable to travel to Germany. They returned to Fowey where a memorial service was to be held in St Fimbarrus Church on February 11, five days after Bevil's death.

Canon Purcell, the old family friend and yacht club associate, conducted the service and many people attended. The sad family group of Q and Lady Quiller-Couch, their daughter Foy and Bevil's fiancée May were isolated in their grief. Life would never be the same again. Their hopes for the future were gone. Q was a broken man who never got over the loss, nor did Lady Quiller-Couch. Foy abandoned her thoughts of marriage and vowed to devote herself to caring for her parents. May remained faithful to Bevil's memory and believed she would never marry.

Agonised over the loss of his son Q decided to resign from his post as Professor at Cambridge in order to be with his wife in Fowey. He wrote: "My time at Cambridge is not likely to be long. The household is so badly broken up that my duty seems to lie at home." Later he did decide, or was persuaded, to return to Cambridge, and there he immersed himself in overwork. He wrote: "It deadens pain. I begin to see that it were better and braver to face the pain for by shirking it one's whole mind gets deadened. Half my time I really don't care what happens in a world that has killed my dearest and most natural hope."

The yacht club management committee met on March 11, 1919. There were five members present and a sad letter was read out from Lady Quiller-Couch and the Commodore, thanking them for their letter of sympathy.

After the 'Great War'

Q faced a bleak future with much courage. Not only did he throw himself into his Cambridge work, but he renewed his literary output and also committed himself to public work for the county. By April 8 he was back in the chair at the yacht club, discussing such ordinary matters as decorating the club for regatta and arranging an inscription for the Airymouse figurehead. There was also discussion resulting in agreement that the club should be responsible for regatta expenses, not the sailing committee.

It seems possible that there were money worries for the club committee. It was decided that officers joining Fowey auxiliary hospital after May 1, 1919 should pay five shillings to cover the period of their stay in hospital. Those who joined the club prior to May 1 would be allowed to continue their free membership. These revisions of the rate were printed on a card and sent to all the hospitals in the town.

1919 was a difficult year for the yacht club as it was for the country as a whole. Whatever the difficulties were though, there was a constant reminder of what had been lost. Almost three-quarters of a million young men had been killed in the war. There were greater losses of young officers than amongst other ranks. A million and a half young men who survived the war were permanently disabled by wounds or the effects of poison gas.

What did it matter that the billiard table was worn out and the lavatory drains blocked once again when the club still guarded the coats and waterproofs of young men who would never return.

On June 10 Q chaired a committee meeting at the club. It had been decided that the town regatta would be held on August 6. The committee did not feel able to give the usual £10 for town fireworks. There was talk of abandoning the club regatta because the peace celebrations were to be held on June 3, 4 and 5.

It was decided that the club carpets be steam cleaned and that the steward be supplied with a new uniform.

After a lapse of nearly four years there was only a partial revival of regatta sailing. The Royal Fowey Yacht Club nor Polruan organised any racing and it was left to Sir Charles Hanson and his committee to organise a one day event for the Town Regatta. On the day there was a light and tricky westward breeze. The Stenalees Silver Band played a programme of music throughout the proceedings, from the committee ship moored midstream. Sailing, rowing and swimming races were followed by a fancy dress carnival and a dance in the evening.

The Peace Celebrations included June 3 which was to have been Bevil and May's wedding day. Q moved his household to a house on Dartmoor to get away from it all. As it was he picked up a newspaper on the day and read of "Boy's" DSO in the Birthday List.

He wrote to his sister Lilian about Bevil's horse. "Peggy is for the present at

Sir Arthur Quiller-Couch brought Bevil's horse, Peggy, back to Fowey after the Great War. Foy Quiller-Couch is photographed here outside the Haven, The Fowey Hotel in the background. Foy rode Peggy regularly always accompanied by Bevil's dog, Jory.

livery opposite Marble Arch. Whether or not she detected something familiar in my footsteps when I went into the loose box she was waiting for me. Took no notice of the stable man but came straight to me, snuffed me all over the chest and then bent down her neck while I stroked her. She nuzzled my wrist and back of my other hand as if kissing it over and over. When I turned to speak to the manager her nose came pushing between my arm and body, kind of insisting that I hadn't made enough love to her. It sounds silly, but it seemed as if the creature really did know something and was trying to say it."

Later on in the year he was able to bring Peggy to Fowey. He arranged pasture and stabling at five shillings a week so she was able to live out her days in peace and green fields.

At the AGM of the yacht club on November 11 Q was re-elected Commodore in his absence. It was announced that the club membership had fallen to 221 and that no less than 1,169 convalescent officers had been entertained at the club during the war.

The Commodore resumed his professional duties at Cambridge at the beginning of the new academic year 1919-1920 and found more students than ever attending his lectures. Cambridge was crowded with young people back from the war eager to catch up with interrupted studies. There was the usual influx from schools. What was new was the number of women. During the war one and a half million women had replaced men in vital employment. Now they were expecting equal educational opportunities also.

It was unthinkable that Q could stop the work that he had pioneered at Cambridge, establishing the English Tripos, the first examination of which was held in 1919. In any case it helped him to immerse himself in hard work even though he lived with ever present sadness. He wrote:

"There are few households in this land that this war has left without a domestic sorrow far more real, more natural, more abiding than any exultation over victory. All the old statues of Victory have wings, but Grief has no wings. She is the unwelcome lodger that squats on the hearth stone between us and the fire and will not move or be dislodged."

Instinctively Q dedicated himself to the youth of the time. Knowing that he could not cherish and celebrate Bevil's children he perhaps found fulfilment with other children in other ways. Not only did he spend the rest of his life at Cambridge teaching undergraduates but he also dedicated his time in Cornwall fostering secondary education for all. He was elected to the newly-formed Cornwall Education Committee and served diligently on that body for 30 years, many of them as chairman.

This pressure of work did not mean that he relinquished his job as Commodore to the yacht club. By April 1920 he was back in the chair planning the regatta for August 20 and sorting out problems in arranging the 'at home' rather than let it be discontinued. The Reverend Danby and Mrs Purcell offered to organise the arrangements. The club was painted in time for the regatta and the billiard table re-covered and new balls obtained.

On August 20, Fowey was en fete when the Royal Fowey Yacht Club Regatta was revived for the first time since 1913. The morning was dull but in the afternoon there was bright sunshine when about 300 guests attended the 'at home' on the terrace. The 'officer of the day' as usual was Q who was assisted by his old friend Herbert Phelps, the secretary of the club. The terrace must have been extremely crowded as the band of the Royal Marines sat around the flagpole and played all afternoon whilst the guests circulated as best they could.

In the evening there was a carnival procession in the town where collections were made for Fowey Cottage Hospital and Nursing Association. Later there was a fancy dress ball in the Armoury. This was the pattern of events for the 1921 regatta also but the joyous times of pre-war regattas seemed to be over.

Although by the AGM the membership had begun to increase, there were very many members who had not paid their subscriptions. The decoration of the club had been very expensive and there was a worrying decline in the club's financial state.

★ ★ ★ ★ ★ ★ ★ ★ ★ ★ ★ ★ ★

The committee hoped to restore 'club life' to that of pre-war years but the regatta of 1922 was disappointing. The Western Morning News wrote:

"The conditions were almost perfect and although the entries for the principal events were disappointing the races for the smaller local boats was as successful as ever. For well over 20 years now this regatta had been attracting entrants from Falmouth and Plymouth and other localities, and on one occasion there had been over 90 boats in the harbour.

"This year, however there were no competitors from Plymouth and only six from Falmouth of which only four started. The small number of entries is generally assigned to the fact that the cost of upkeep and manning of the larger yachts is now considerably higher than it was a few years ago, and the disappointment of the yacht club seems likely to be shared by other clubs in the West."

Nationally there was a decline in prosperity as unemployment increased and major industries were dislocated as a result of the war. The decline in the fortunes of the RFYC was a reflection of this and income fell. To make matters worse, a serious deficit in bar takings was found to be because the steward was drinking the gin. He confessed his responsibility for the loss of profits. He was given a chance to rehabilitate himself and to continue in the job. The loss was written off. The club struggled on. It was resolved to elect the manager of Barclays Bank to the post of Honorary Treasurer. This was presumably in order to have a professional supervising the club accounts. There is no mention of payment for fulfilling these duties. Perhaps the honour of election was considered sufficient reward. Succeeding Barclays Bank managers found the RFYC commitment to be an obligatory function when taking up the new position managing the bank in Fowey.

The 1922 regatta was well-supported by spectators and the weather was fine. Although there were few entries for the race for yachts over seven tons, there were many yachts entering the smaller races. This was a significant trend here and elsewhere as yachting became more available as a sport that was no longer confined to the extremely wealthy.

Q wrote to a friend and described the regatta:

"This house is much exposed to guests visiting just now, and moreover Regatta Week is upon us. You did know that I was Commodore didn't you. Time was when I used to enjoy this sort of thing- firing guns and starting yacht races and once a day, I being laden and accoutred with two guns, stop watch, megaphone, cartridge bag and what-not, was asked by a very rich man at the club landing steps "Do you enjoy this sort of thing?"

"Well," says I "now you speak of it, I suppose I do, in a simple way"

"Then you're a lucky fellow" says he, for I've been chasing pleasure these 40 years and haven' caught up with it yet."

But the figure of Grief that Q described sitting on his hearth stone was still there. Q continued the sequel to the conversation "that man made a good end. His yacht foundered in the Bay of Biscay and all took to the boats in bitter weather, and made land somewhere. But he was dead, frozen stiff when they lifted him out, having shed his oilskin coat to wrap up his small child. He was the lucky fellow after all. He could save his boy." What agony that Q could not save his.

A week or so later in another letter he wrote:

"The regatta went off in a grand weather and the sea like champagne. I got away fifteen boats in one of the prettiest starts ever seen. After which my wife and I received the rank and fashion on the Club Terrace to the strains of the Royal Marines, who played with extreme virtuosity through a programme of the world's very worst music.... Space will not allow me to tell you of a dance, a carnival procession and another race in which my daughter sailed against

"My daughter sailed against 14 competitors and came in third." Jigsaw, *built for* Loftus Long *by* Watty *in 1906. Sold to Miss Foy Quiller-Couch in 1923 and sailed by her thereafter.*

fourteen competitors and came in third."

By the end of 1926 it was decided to obtain quotations for the installation of electric lights in the club. Until then it had been illuminated by gas and oil lamps. Concern was expressed at how this would be paid for as there were severe money problems. The steward had resigned earlier in the year because of a fall in bar profits which had been due to his inaccurate accounts of bar takings which included watering the gin. It was necessary to buy crockery, cutlery, plates and table linen and a storage cupboard. A new suit and uniform for the new steward was also needed.

It was decided to issue new debentures and to increase income by raising subscriptions. Until these were implemented the club had continuing money worries. At the AGM in 1927 it was stated that it could no longer make ends meet

---

BAR PRICES - 1926

Whisky (small) plain or with splash 7d
Whisky (large) plain or with splash 1s 2d
Gin (small) plain or with bitters 7d
Gin and Vermouth or mixed Vermouth 8d
Sherry 7d
Port (small) 8d
Port (large) 1/-
Brandy 10d
Beers and Stouts 6d
Minerals 3d
Soda water (bottles) 3d
Tonic water, Schweppes dry ginger ale .... 4½ d
Prices per bottle
Whisky 12s 6d
Gin 11s 6d
Sherry 7/-
Port 7s 6d
Brandy 18/-

Beers and Stouts .... 5/6 per dozen

Cases 4/- each – bottles returnable
Minerals 3/- per dozen

---

on the present income. The regatta had showed a loss even though the 'at home' had been a social success as usual although there had been fewer race entries and from the large vessels in particular.

These were hard times for the nation. The post war boom had not lasted. The General Strike in 1926 had highlighted the despair of the working man but it brought no respite from long hours and low wages. Quite the reverse, after the strike many had to return to work for lower wages than before.

In 1928 the committee agreed that they were unable to subscribe money to help the town regatta. The Commodore and Honorary Secretary volunteered £10 each to ensure the regatta fund against loss. An individual member agreed to pay the cost of electric light installation.

The membership in 1928 increased by four to 220. Mr L P Mendels was elected In-Port member and Sir Gerald du Maurier was elected Out- Port member. He was a famous actor and theatre manager living with his family in Hampstead and owning a holiday home in Fowey at Ferryside.

Gradually things improved and by the time of the next AGM in 1929 the Treasurer reported that the financial situation was satisfactory. Structurally though the club was showing signs of deterioration. In 1930 the roof was in need of repair and in 1931 the steward's bedroom floor gave way because the boards and joists were rotten. It was also necessary to cover the billiard table at a cost of £30.

A. cheery atmosphere !

Regatta programmes changed very little during the 1930s.

PROGRAMME OF MUSIC.

MARCH } POT POURRI }	" Passing of the Regiments "	*Aubrey Winter*
SELECTION ...	" Student Prince " ...	*Romberg*
VALSE MEDLEY	" Golden Valse " ...	*Aubrey Winter*
NOVELTY CHARACTERISTIC }	"Teddy Bear's Picnic " ...	*J. Bratton*
FOX TROT	"There's Something about a Soldier "	*Noel Gay*
SELECTION ...	" Rose Marie "	...*Friml & Stothart*
TONE PICTURE ...	" Sunset Glow "	*Ketelby*
INDIAN INTERMEZZO	" Aisha " ...	*John Lindsey*
INCIDENTAL MUSIC } TO THE PLAY }	" Monsieur Beaucaire " ...	*John Bucalossi*
TWO STEP ...	" I lost my heart in Heidleberg "	*F. Raymond*
SELECTION ...	" Desert Song " ...	*Romberg*
MUSICAL ...	" Comedy Switch " ...	*Henry Hall*
SELECTION ...	" Fredrica " ...	*Lehar*
SELECTION ...	" Cavalcade " ...	*Noel Coward*
	" Regimental "	

THE KING.

Band Master—MR. G. P. ROBINSON.

Royal Fowey Yacht Club

REGATTA

Tuesday, September 5th, 1933

By kind permission of Major A. C. Rolston and Officers
The Band of the
DEVON & CORNWALL (FORTRESS) ROYAL ENGINEERS
will play during the afternoon

JORY, PRINTER, FOWEY.

FLAG OFFICERS:

COMMODORE	-	Sir Arthur Quiller-Couch, J.P.
VICE-COMMODORE	-	G. T. Petherick, J.P.
REAR-COMMODORE	-	Col. Edward Treffry

C.M.G., O.B,E., A.D.C., D.L.

SAILING COMMITTEE:

D. R. Carter,	Dr. J. S. Moore,
E. E. English,	M. E. Negus,
W. V. G. Hancock	Col. T. W. Simpson,
W. B. S. Hawkins,	J. L. Toyne,
J. E. S. Long,	

A. W. Burghard, Hon. Sec.

Q RACE   Start 10.15 a.m.

Handicap for Yachts exceeding 16 tons T.M.

Entrance fee 10/-   Course 18 miles.

First Prize, £10   Second, £4   Third, £2

RECALL NO.	YACHT	RIG	TONS T.M.	OWNER
5	Primrose	Schr.	32	E. Schalburg
2	Rosemary IV.	Bmu. Slp.	25	Isaac Bell
3	Lady Edith	Slp.	31	Maj. B. H. Piercy
4	Makora	Cut.	20	W. R. Macpherson
10	Veronique	Yawl.	33	Col. E. Treffry
1	Dorina	Cut.	50	J. S. Highfield

HANDICAP—Dorina scratch ; allows Rosemary IV, 25 mins. ; Lady Edith and Primrose 31 mins. ; Veronique 45 mins. ; Makora, 60 mins.

E RACE   Start 10.15 a.m.

Race for Yachts of the International 12 Metre Class.

Entrance fee 10/-   First Prize, £12 12s.   Second, £7 7s.   Course 18 miles.

RECALL NO.	YACHT	NO. ON SAIL	OWNER

R RACE   Start 10.30 a.m.

Handicap for Yachts exceeding 7 tons but not exceeding 16

Tons T.M.   Entrance fee 5/-   Course 18 miles.

RECALL NO.	YACHT	RIG	TONS T.M.	OWNER
1	Aline IV.	Cut.	10	C. H. Waugh
2	Veronique	Bmu. Slp.	8	O. F. Gayson
3	Osprey	Cut.	13	P. M. Holman
4	Mayfly	Bmu. Slp.	8	Harley Mead

HANDICAP—Mayfly scratch ; allows Aline IV 16 mins. ; Osprey 18 mins. ; Veronique 30 mins.

PROGRAMME OF MUSIC.

1	MARCH	" Villefranche "	Francis Popey
2	OVERTURE,	" Bohemian Girl "	Balfe
3	SELECTION	" Waltzes from Vienna "	Johann Strauss
4	VALSE	" Columbine "	Cyril G. Gardiner
5	FOX TROT	" Lies "	Harry Barris
6	DERVISH CHORUS	" In the Soudan "	G. Sebek
7	PICCOLO SOLO	" The Wren "	E. Damare

Musician W. TULLE.

8	GRAND SELECTION	" Faust "	Gounod
9	MEDLEY VALSE	" The Costume Ball "	Aubrey Winter
10	SELECTION	" Maid of the Mountains "	Frazer Simpson
11	INTERMEZZO	" In a Persian Market "	Ketelby
12	POTPOURRI	" Old and New "	Herman Finck
13	SELECTION	" Lilac Time "	Schubert
14	WALTZ	" For You "	J. Burke
15	HUMOROUS MARCH	" O, Ihr Weiber "	Paul Lincke
		" Regimental "	

THE KING.

CONDUCTOR : MR. G. P. ROBINSON.

Royal Fowey Yacht Club.

REGATTA

————

TUESDAY, September 6th., 1932.

————

By kind permission of
Major A. Rolston and Officers
THE BAND OF THE DEVON (FORTRESS) ROYAL ENGINEERS
will play during the afternoon.

FLAG OFFICERS :

COMMODORE	-	-	Sir Arthur Quiller-Couch, J.P.
VICE-COMMODORE	-	-	G. T. Petherick, J.P.
REAR-COMMODORE	-	-	Col. Edward Treffry,

C.M.G., O.B.E., A.D.C., D.L.

SAILING COMMITTEE :

Rev. C. E. Danby,   M. E. Negus,

E. E. English,   Col. T. W. Simpson,

W. V. G. Hancock,   J. L. Toyne,

W. B. S. Hawkins,   Dr. J. S. Moore,

J. E. S. Long,

A. W. Burghard, Hon. Sec.

B RACE   Start 3.30 p.m.

Race for one design "Troy" Class

Inside Harbour   Entrance fee 1/-

First Prize, £2   Second, £1   Third, 10/-

This Race will be sailed under the Rules framed for this Class

YACHT	OWNER	NO. ON SAIL
Jocelyn	Sir Chas. Hanson	1
Anemone	J. A. S. Strong	2
Janet	Dr. Moore	3
Shimmer	Col. E. Treffry	4
Amethyst	S. J. Samuel	5
Ruby	{ W. H. Graham	6
	{ T. Warne	

1 Race for Yachts' Punts

Oarsman and boat to belong to the same Yacht.

First, £1   Second, 10/-   Third, 5/-

**2 Race for Four-oared Boats not exceeding 18 feet overall
and not less than 5 feet 6 inches beam.**

First, £3 Second, £1   Third, 10/-

Q's later years

Q celebrated his 60th birthday on November 21 1923 just after the AGM of the Yacht Club when he was once again elected Commodore. He chaired most of the yacht club committee meetings but had to delegate when his duties in Cambridge prevented him from attending.

His job as Professor of English Literature was a life appointment. There was to be no retirement and he continued to actively serve the post until his death.

The job was no sinecure. He lectured regularly and was so popular that lecture theatres were crowded with students standing. He was much in demand in Cambridge by clubs and societies and was Commodore of the Cambridge University Cruising Club.

His flood of literary work continued whether he was in Cambridge or Fowey.

At the age of 60 Q had a smooth unlined face. He had a ready smile. He described himself when a youngster as a 'small stout fellow covered with variegated freckles' but by the time he was 60 his red hair had turned white. His once luxuriant

Sir Arthur Quiller-Couch

moustache was clipped close. Five foot in height and slim his posture was still as erect as it have ever been.

Contemporaries commented that he was never in a hurry and never ill tempered. He was always fond of bright colours and wore a variety of coloured waistcoats with loud checked shirts when a student at Oxford. A fellow student recalls Q's tutor reproaching him. "What *another* new pair of trarsers, Mr Couch?"

A rival commented that "He arrived at Cambridge dressed like a racing tout". His many pieces of luggage always included several hat boxes containing a range of different coloured bowler hats to co-ordinate with his many coloured outfits.

Q never seemed to tire during his vacations in Fowey away from his duties in Cambridge. Not only did he serve on Cornwall Education Committee for thirty years but he also served as a Justice of the Peace sitting at Petty Sessions in Tywardreath near Fowey. For twenty one years he was Chairman of the Fowey

Q's friend Colonel Edward Treffry was made Mayor of Fowey in 1936.

Harbour Commissioners. He was also a Trinity House Pilotage Sub Commissioner.

It was in 1912 that Fowey became a borough again. The petition to the Crown was presented by Q and Charles Treffry of Place. In October 1913 the MP for South East Cornwall, Sir Reginald Pole Carew handed over the new charter to Charles Treffry, the first Mayor of the revived borough. The ceremony was held in the grounds of Place under a chestnut tree.

In Q's speech on that occasion he said

"Although our streets are narrow our minds may be broad enough to keep our sense of proportion and to remember that our borough is too small to allow for quarrellings whether religious or political, or to admit to any other rivalry save in the service of Fowey".

In 1936 Charles' son Edward Treffry became Mayor.

In the following November 1937 Q himself was elected Mayor. It was an occasion that he greatly enjoyed and so did the town.

His old Cambridge friend Freddy Brittain wrote:

"As he walked along the narrow street of the diminutive borough, whether to Mr Rickard the barber for his morning shave in Fore Street, to the Town Hall to discuss business with the Town Clerk, or to the yacht club to choose the prizes or music for the regatta, he was greeted all the way and stopped every few yards to speak to someone or other. There were people of every walk of life. Whoever they were he treated them all with the same grave courtesy and their attitude to him was deferential without being in the least servile. According to their degree of intimacy with him some addressed his as plain "Sir", some as "Sir Arthur", some as "Q" and some as "Your Worship." No visitor would have been surprised to hear him addressed as "Your Majesty", for Fowey seemed to be a miniature kingdom and Q its king."

When Q celebrated his 70th birthday on November 21 1933, he was in better health than 10 years before and his eyesight had improved. Although he described himself as a certifiable old man he was still young at heart.

He organised the regatta and the town's celebrations with as much energy as ever. Never tired he would celebrate that end of the festivities at the fair on the town quay riding a merry-go-round horse in evening dress with cigar in mouth and a wave and a laugh.

In 1933 he resigned his post as Chairman of the Education Committee and his office as County Alderman. He had served both for almost thirty years.

His enthusiasm for Fowey, his home and the harbour, never flagged and his continuing role as Commodore of the Yacht Club was never in doubt.

Q wrote:

"A heavenly summer down here. Many more visitors than ever, but the balance almost redeemed by the slightness of their clothing.

"On the eve of the regatta with three of the great racers here, Candida, Astra and Westward and heaps of others, the harbour all be-jewelled of nights."

A month later he wrote:

"Oh these visitors! But now at least they are clearing out and taking their brats back to school. And now above an empty harbour we are wrestling with a plum and apple crop the like of which I have never known. Five afternoons have we worked in the hot sun and gathered a quarter of the crop, if so much. What a summer too, but not torrid here. The grass is quite green and the fuchsias in great bloom."

Q always travelled by train and never owned a motor car. His return to his other life in Cambridge required much planning and co-operation with station masters and the delivery of masses of flowers to his room, all ordered by telegram from a florist in Cambridge. His rooms were always filled with vases and bowls of flowers and Peonies and Chrysanthemums were his favourites.

His friend Freddy Brittain lived on the same staircase at Jesus College, Cambridge.

He describes in his book, entitled simply, 'Q' some of their rituals:

"When his guests had gone he would devote himself to work until bed time. He like to have company while undressing ~ an operation that he performed from below upwards. As he took off each garment he folded it carefully and carried it into his bedroom talking all the time. His undressing was a miniature drama with exits, entrances, speeches and now and then a hoarse stage whisper from behind the scenes when he dropped a stud or jabbed his toe against a piece of furniture.

"If he had been out to a feast he looked a particularly strange sight when he stood barefoot but otherwise in complete evening dress, stranger still when having disappeared into the wings to put away his trousers he reappeared and stood framed in the doorway of his bedroom, barelegged with shirt tails hanging down under his white waistcoat and tail coat. When he had got into his pyjamas he sat down by the fire for a last cigarette and then dismissed his guest.

"Within a very few minutes of getting into bed he was fast asleep under a copy of John Speed's map of Cornwall with its dolphins blowing full rigged ships along the English Channel home to Fowey".

Half a minute to go —

Kathleen —

WILD CAT, MARIONETTE, and Florence —

Urbane fisherman (to maddened officials, after eight hours of a southerly roll) 'J see you have brought up for some time ? Good sport, gentlemen, J trust ?

The old 'LAIS' passing through the small fry —

Some popular yachts in Fowey in the 1930s.

1933. Veronique. *Owned by Col. Edward Treffry, Rear-Commodore of R.F.Y.C.*

Estelle *in 1934. Owned by Major T.C. Thorn, M.C. A regular visitor to Fowey.*

1934. Zoraida II. *Owned by J.H. Stokes.*

Britannia and the Greyhounds of the Sea

Queen Victoria's eldest son, Edward Prince of Wales, enjoyed sailing. He was born in 1841 and did not become King until 1901 when he was sixty years of age. Although the Victorian Era was known for its staid virtues, the Prince of Wales was known for his extravagance, recreational pursuits and self-indulgence. One of the highlights of the year was racing at Cowes when many of the crowned heads of Europe brought their yachts and moored them in the harbour. With Queen Victoria in residence at Osborne House, Cowes was like a second court.

The Prince of Wales became embroiled in competition with his German relatives who were having large and expensive boats built with which they intended to beat all comers.

As a result the Prince of Wales had *Britannia* built in 1893. She was designed by G L Watson and built in the Clyde yard of D and W Henderson. This was a very large boat of 211 tons with a mast of 110 feet and overall length of 102 feet.

It took fifteen crew members on deck to haul the mainsail whilst others climbed the rat lines and swung across onto the halyard. The sail area was 10,000 square feet in total and it took two hours to prepare her for the starting gun when racing.

She was designed for racing and in 1895 she won 33 first prizes out of 39 starts. By 1935 she had won 200 first prizes.

King Edward VII gave his name to the Edwardian Era. His reign was short and he died in 1910 at the age of 68.

His son George V inherited, along with the throne, the now celebrated yacht *Britannia*. Having been trained in the Royal Navy King George V was a much more serious sailor than his father. He employed Sir Philip Hunloke perhaps the finest helmsman in the world to win races on *Britannia*, whatever the weather. During forty four years *Britannia* 's rig was changed and improved seven times.

For rich and poor alike the competition between the great ocean racers of the day the Royal Yacht *Britannia* was a matter of intense interest.

National fascination with yachting continued. For the poor the competition between the ocean racers of the time focused on the royal yacht *Britannia*. Yacht clubs sprang up along the coats as those with money enough emulated the wealthy sailors of the day albeit on a smaller scale. In 1900 yachting was included as a sport in the second modern Olympic Games.

Sir Thomas Lipton had made a fortune selling tea to the British. He had built a series of yachts all named *Shamrock* in the hope of winning the America's Cup. In all there were five *Shamrocks* and although Sir Thomas Lipton, never won the America's Cup his exploits provided excellent publicity for the tea business.

The America's Cup race was cancelled in 1914 when war broke out and ocean racing was not resumed until 1921.

Sir Thomas Lipton's *Shamrock V* was intended to be his last challenge for the

America's Cup and it was agreed to build it to the American Universal Rule which was a simplification of the complicated regulations that had developed.

The result was the J class yacht considered to be the most beautiful yacht design up to that time. Only ten J class yachts were ever built. They were huge boats between 76 and 87 feet at the waterline. The masts were over 160 feet. The mainsails were made of cotton in vast sail lofts and each weighed a ton.

The flying jib was equal in size to that of the mainsail of a 39 foot boat. Spinnakers measured up to 18,000 square feet.

King George V approved of the development of the J Class boats. He engaged the greatest designer of ocean yachts of the time Charles Nicholson to adapt the spars and sails of *Britannia* to compete with the modern boats. Once underway the momentum of these huge vessels would carry them for miles even in light airs. *Britannia* could cope with heavier weather than the modern boats and it was said that with a fresh breeze thrumming through her rigging there was an unforgettable sonorous drone like a huge double bass.

Britannia was now able to go "like a scalded cat" and did well in competition. J boats raced between 1920 and 1937. *Britannia* was not fitted out in 1929 because of the illness of King George V. However, on July 18, 1930 he was racing in his boat at Falmouth. At the Summer General Meeting of the Royal Cornwall Yacht Club in Falmouth, the following messages was telegraphed to the King:

> "The flag officers and members of the Royal Cornwall Yacht Club desire to submit their loyal duty to their Royal Patron King George V and to offer their humble congratulations to his Majesty on the occasion of his winning with his yacht *Britannia* her 199th victory at their regatta on 18th July last."

It was in the following year of 1931 that the J boats came to Cornwall. The Royal Cornwall Yacht Club arranged a special race on July 17. This meant that the J boats and the old yachts of the 76ft rating and above would compete against each other. In fact only four boats competed: *Britannia* (HM The King); *Astra* (Hugh F Paul); *Candida* (H A Andreae) and Sir Thomas Lipton's new boat *Shamrock V*. Unlike the success of the previous year, *Britannia* gave up as did *Candida*.

Sir Thomas Lipton died in 1931 at the age of eighty but his boat *Shamrock V* was bought and raced by Sir T O M Sopwith, an aircraft manufacturer. He had dreams of winning the America's Cup and engaged Charles Nicholson to design and build *Endeavour* and *Endeavour II*.

The J boat race in Falmouth was cancelled in 1932 but in 1933 it was held once again and four boats competed: *Shamrock V* (T O M Sopwith); was the winner whilst *Astra* (Hugh F Paul) came second and the King's *Britannia* came third. The fourth competitor was W L Stephenson's new boat *Velsheda*.

Velsheda was built by Camper and Nicholson of Gosport for the Woolworth's millionaire W L Stephenson.

She was 127 feet overall and 83 feet at the water line. She carried 7,600 square feet

The start of the J Class race, 27 June 1935. The King's yacht K1 Britannia is to the right of the picture. The Gribbin shows in the background.

The Greyhounds of the Sea moored off Fowey, 27 June 1935.

The King's yacht Britannia *at Fowey 1935.*

Endeavour *off Fowey 1935*.

of sail and her steel hull displaced 205 tons.

Once again it was planned that the Royal Cornwall Yacht Club in Falmouth should invite the J boats in 1934, however there was some opposition to the proposal. Perhaps this was because some members found the custom of raising over £100 in prize money by subscription too expensive. The dissenters were overruled. Moreover, Mr T O M Sopwith and designer Charles Nicholson were keen to try out the new boat *Endeavour*. They requested a course which included a long beat to windward in open sea. The race was arranged for June 29 and there were six competitors. *Astra* (Hugh F. Paul) was the winner, *Britannia* (HM The King) second, and *Candida* (H A Andreae) third. The other three entries were placed as follows:

> *Endeavour* (T O M Sopwith) fourth; *Shamrock V* (C R Fairey) fifth; and *Velsheda* (W L Stephenson) sixth.

There must have been great satisfaction in the Royal Fowey Yacht Club when it was agreed that in the summer of 1935 the J class boats would race from Fowey.

The planning for the J class race began with a special committee meeting at the Royal Fowey Yacht Club which was held on October 11, 1934. The financial position of the club was by then satisfactory and it was agreed to offer prize money of £70 first prize, £25 second, and £15 third prize.

Initially it was suggested that there would be a dinner on the evening of the race at a cost of £1 per head to which ladies would be invited. Instead there was a sherry party. Admission was by ticket at a cost of 2/6. Security at the club was ensured by the presence of two policemen, one at each entrance to the club.

The Western Morning News announced:

> "Never before in the history of yachting have all the boats of the J fleet been anchored in such close proximity."

> "Seven boats were entered for the race. The weather proved ideal for the inaugural visit of the J boats to Fowey. Thousands of sightseers poured into the town. The wind was fresh SW by W. The fields above the harbour were crowded with visitors and ice cream vendors. The race was due to start at 10.30am. The officer of the day was Rear Commodore Colonel Edward Treffry. He was assisted by Colonel T W Simpson, J E S Long, J L Toyne, M E Negus, J Blowey (timekeeper) and D R Carter".

The newspaper account continues:

> "*Britannia* was first to come out of the harbour with her glossy black sides and snow white deck, flying her red and blue racing flag. She was followed by the pale blue *Shamrock* and *Yankee* which had a white hull. The boats presented an imposing spectacle as they manoeuvred at the start. A good sailing breeze drove the yachts at a fine speed as they set off on the first leg west towards Mevagissey. The course was a triangular one to be completed twice with a total of 30.5 miles.

> "The race was won by *Endeavour* (T O M Sopwith) in just under 3.5 hours. W

L Stephenson's *Velsheda* came home second seven minutes later sailed by her designer Charles Nicholson. *Shamrock* was third, closely followed by *Yankee*. The Royal Yacht *Britannia* had a disappointing race. She was lagging 15 minutes behind when she lost the sheets of her double clewed jib. At this point she abandoned the race.

"The next day all the boats competing in the J class arrived in Falmouth. The race under the auspices of the Royal Cornwall Yacht Club took place on June 28. There were six competitors. The winner was *Astra*. Second came *Endeavour* with *Shamrock* third, *Velsheda* fourth and *Yankee* fifth. Once again *Britannia* faced disappointment and had to give up the race".

★ ★ ★ ★ ★ ★ ★ ★ ★ ★ ★ ★

It was early in the following year on January 20, 1936 that King George V died aged almost 70. He had been on the throne for 25 years. He was succeeded by his son Edward VIII. King Edward VIII had no interest in the sport of sailing. *Britannia* was scuttled during 1936 in deep waters off Cowes.

She was stripped of her gear which was sold at auction. Her Norway fir spinnaker boom became a flag staff on Carisbrook Castle. Her Oregon pine mast was erected at Dartmouth. Her burgees were presented by King Edward VIII to the clubs in whose regattas she had raced so hard. £1,050, the proceeds of the sale were presented to the National Memorial Fund to King George V.

On July 8th *Britannia*, a garland of wild flowers around her prow was towed by two destroyers away from her berth in the Medina. Watching over her were Sir Philip Hunloke, Captain Turner her Skipper, the Kings Steward and an old pensioner from Portsmouth. Fifty seven years after her launch a hole was blown in her bow and she swiftly sank.

Britannia's last great season was in 1931. The heyday of the J class boat was shortlived. The cost of maintaining these extravagant boats had become prohibitive and without the old royal competition J class racing was in decline and within three years only four boats were still competing.

However the Royal Fowey Yacht Club were keen to host a J class race as they had the year before. This was in spite of the fact that maintenance expenses at the club were accumulating. Winter gales had damaged the club roof and the chimney stack and the plaster ceiling in the hall had fallen down. Nevertheless, plans were in hand for a J class race to be held on June 27, 1936.

It was hoped to hold a sherry party for about 200 guests and a letter had been sent round the membership inviting subscriptions to pay for it all. Party invitations were to be sent to the Mayor and the harbour master and also to any commanders of HM ships in harbour at the time.

There were special races in Falmouth for the J boats on June 24 and 25 but only four boats entered: T O M Sopwith's *Endeavour II* which won, Hugh F Paul's *Astra* which came second, then W L Stephenson's *Velsheda* followed by H A Andreae's *Endeavour I*.

The next day the same four boats raced at Fowey. This time *Astra* won and *Endeavour I* came second.

The glory days of J class racing were over. The Fowey race was disappointing and the event was not a success. What was worst the cost of the sherry party was not even covered by the sale of tickets and ran at a loss of £7 2s 3d.

Life at the club soon returned to normal though, and the regatta was planned for September 1, 1936. Members were asked to subscribe to the costs of the Regatta and the Sailing Committee to grant £100 for prizes. As well as the repair work to the damage from winter storms expense was also incurred because of the building of a ladies cloak room.

At the AGM that year the club as reported to be in a sound financial position. Sir Arthur Quiller-Couch was re-elected Commodore and a motion was passed "that ladies could only be brought onto the club front and into the lounge and nowhere else".

Meanwhile Hitler had re-occupied the Rhineland. Tension was rising in Europe as were the fears of war.

The pattern of club activities continued through 1937 and 1938 much as before. The Commodore chaired as many meetings as he could, a surprising number considering his academic duties in Cambridge.

Structural problems continued particularly as a result of more winter storms and the club's exposed site at the waters edge. At the AGM on November 10, 1938 it was reported that finances of the club were satisfactory. There had been a slight fall in membership. Sir Arthur Quiller-Couch was re-elected Commodore.

The 1939 Regatta was planned for August 28, but was cancelled at the last moment.

The Second World War

On September 1 1939 Germany invaded Poland and by September 3 Britain was once again at war with Germany.

By October the yacht club was closing at 9.30 because of restrictions on the use of electricity and fuel.

Attempts were made to provide efficient 'blackout' for the reading room. It was not possible to have all the lights burning and members complained that they couldn't see to read. In February 1940 it was reported that efficient blackout for the reading room would cost £5. It was decided to postpone this expense until the autumn as Daylight Saving Time was to start at the end of the month.

Access ladders to the shore were removed and barbed wire covered the terrace railings. A stirrup pump for fighting fires was acquired and arrangements were made for the air raid warden to have a duplicate key to the club premises in case of emergency.

As during the first World War the yacht club became a social club much frequented by officers who were stationed in Fowey. It had been recommended that subscriptions from Out Port members should be suspended for the duration of the war.

Officers in Fowey were invited to become temporary members of the club for a fee of five shillings for six months. They were asked to sign the book giving their regiment and to pay at the time of entry. Efforts to blackout the billiard room efficiently had been necessary as billiards was a popular game amongst the officers. Soon the billiard table was showing signs of wear and tear. Although the overall membership numbers had fallen the club flourished financially probably due to increased bar profits.

In a letter to friends Q wrote in 1939:

"I have been kept here by various duties, Fowey having become a garrison town with such a bewildering number of units scattered around. ORFA, RAF, RE. Some yeomanry, half a line battalion not to mention the Navy, and myself the one handy JP sitting and representing Peace in the centre of the small cyclone. A German broadcast the other day announced that Fowey was again in flames. Which it aint and hasn't been. Dr Goebbels must have heard of Troy for the first time and got history mixed up."

"Noise has everywhere invaded this haven - speed boat on patrol, gun practice, siren warnings, bombs and military cyclists hurrying."

Whitehouse beach and Readymoney beach were obstructed by barbed wire and anti-landing concrete posts blocked the quays and slipways. An air raid siren was installed on the top of the church tower. Q wrote:

"We go about our business surrounded by the navy and army in numbers with cannon to the right of us, ditto to left of us and a Bren gun in the next garden."

Fowey Harbour was heavily defended. The harbour entrance was heavily mined. Readymoney Cove was blockaded by an old schooner 'Helena Anna' which later broke up on the beach in a gale. A harbour boom from Polruan Castle to the old Fowey Blockhouse blocked the harbour entrance. A heavy steel net hung from large steel buoys on the surface. Only permitted vessels were allowed through when the boom was opened. Gun emplacements defended the harbour both from the headlands and within the harbour too.

Invasion seemed imminent. Public air raid shelters were opened in Fowey and by August 6 a cellar under the Haven was in use as an air raid shelter. Q himself had a lucky escape from a bombing raid that August. He was working in his garden which he called the Farm on the bank of the river behind Prime Cellars when four bombs fell near enough to knock him to the ground unhurt. Although Cambridge was exposed to air attack also, after the first two or three nights in College air raid shelters, Q would always remain in his bed.

Although he continued working both in Cambridge and Fowey the Commodore was by now a little stooped and frail although his brain was as clear as ever. He returned to Fowey for his 80th birthday celebrations and received hundreds of letters of congratulations. He was in attendance at the club AGM on November 29, 1943 one week later when he was once more elected Commodore.

His old friend Colonel Edward Treffry had died in 1942 and it had been decided not to elect a successor for the time being. The Vice Commodore Mr G T Petherick had died in 1941 and Colonel Treffry had been elected to take his place. Mr M E Negus was elected Rear Commodore.

Q chaired the next two meetings and then returned to Cambridge but he was ill with mouth trouble and could not eat or hold his beloved pipe. He revived a little on his return to Fowey. He presided over the AGM of the Fowey Cottage Hospital and also a committee meeting of the yacht club. Then on March 23 it is said he stumbled in the street avoiding a jeep when he was walking from the Haven to the yacht club. He cut his head and was badly shaken. From then his health deteriorated rapidly but he was back chairing the yacht club committee on April 10 when it was decided to repaint the kitchen. Soon after the meeting Q was so weak he had to take to his bed.

One month later on May 12 when Fowey and the country for miles around was packed with troops and the harbour and its inlets crowded with ships all waiting in tense silence for the signal to invade France, Q died.

Three days later he was carried from the Haven to St Fimbarrus Church in Fowey by six naval men. Behind his coffin walked his boatman/gardener and friend Joseph Welch who carried a bunch of pink valerian and lilac. Behind him walked Lady Quiller-Couch, her daughter Foy and niece Mrs Symondson. Hundreds of people followed, many carrying valerian which Q had called the Pride of Fowey.

D-Day

Three weeks later Fowey harbour suddenly emptied. The long weeks of preparation for the invasion of occupied France were over. The landing craft and their support vessels set sail for Normandy when the Allies open their Second Front and started the liberation of France. The date was June 6, 1944 and was known as D Day.

Although the club was no longer able to function as a Yacht Club in 1944 it continued to be popular as a social club particularly for wounded service personnel who were convalescing in hotels around the town.

From the summer of 1943 life in Fowey had been greatly disrupted by the preparations for the invasion of France.

The harbour and its hinterland were selected as an ideal location for the Advanced Amphibious Base. The function of this unit was to train boat crews and to maintain and repair supporting ships and landing crafts. Several thousand men were trained in Fowey during the time leading to the invasion.

As well as the large numbers of Americans who manned the Advanced Amphibious Training unit, there were a great many medical personnel involved in the United States Hospital Training School at Greenbank Hotel. One hundred and fifty medical officers and 2,850 corpsmen received training in Fowey. It was expected that there would be a great many casualties after the invasion.

The Royal Air Force had a base in Fowey for target testing and target training. A number of British Army Units were based in Fowey also.

As Q described "the air, seas and land were full of men, machinery and noise".

In spite of this disruption he and his management committee strove to provide a degree of continuity at the Yacht Club in spite of its enforced change of use.

Although he was old and frail Q's death must have seemed to mark the end of the world as it had been understood. The fate of the nations was in the balance and the future was unknown in spite of everyone's hopes for victory.

Perhaps it was to show faith in the future that in the summer of 1944 Captain John Treffry offered to the club the purchase of the freehold.

The management committee were unanimous in gratefully accepting this most generous offer. Q would have been pleased. Messrs Graham and Couch dealt with the transfer of deeds and Barclays Bank agreed to take on the trusteeship at a nominal fee of one guinea.

It was decided to establish a memorial fund to commemorate Sir Arthur Quiller-Couch's time as Commodore.

The Annual General Meeting of 1944 was held on November 14. Seventeen members were present and they stood for a minute's silence in memory of Q. He had been Commodore of the Yacht Club for thirty three years.

It was reported that there was now a membership of 33 In Port members and 102 Out Port members.

A suggestion was made that the election of a new Commodore be deferred until the end of the war when there would be a greater number of members present and a more extensive choice of flag officers. This was rejected and it was decided to approach General Browning to ask him if he would be prepared to accept the rôle.

The du Mauriers

General Browning had been elected to the Yacht Club as an Out Port member in January 1935, nearly three years after his marriage to Daphne du Maurier. His father-in-law Sir Gerald du Maurier had been elected to membership seven years before in 1928.

Sir Gerald du Maurier was a successful actor manager who lived with his family in Hampstead. In 1926 he had just staged yet another successful production in the West End and decided to buy a holiday home in the South West although he left the search for a suitable property to his wife.

Lady du Maurier and her daughters came first to Bodinnick and there they found Swiss Cottage overlooking the Fowey Estuary. It may have been somewhat dilapidated but its setting is so beautiful that they bought it. There was money enough to fit it out comfortably in time for a family holiday the next year. For Daphne it was love at first sight and from then on she stayed in Fowey as often as she could. Once the family returned to London she would stay in Fowey returning each day to the holiday home which they had renamed Ferryside. It was in these early days at Fowey that she wrote her first book 'The Loving Spirit'.

Gerald had a motor cruiser built and although he had joined the Yacht Club it was Daphne who showed the greatest interest in sailing. In the company of Harry Adams, her father's boatman, she learned to handle boats, to helm a fishing lugger and to fish. She also learned from him the history of the Slade family, their Polruan boatyard and the building of the schooner *Jane Slade*.

These stories became the basis for the book 'The Loving Spirit' which became an instant success.

General Browning was known as Boy or Tommy to his friends. He had first come to Fowey from the sea when he sailed in on his motor cruiser *Ygdrasil* accompanied by a friend. The pair were dashing young officers come to investigate the young author of a book that Tommy had just read. The year was 1931, the book was 'The Loving Spirit' and the young author was Daphne du Maurier, then aged 25. Tommy was 35 and the son of a military family. He had been educated at Eton and Sandhurst and served in the Grenadier Guards. He had won the DSO at the age of 20 during the First World War, and also the Croix du Guerre. Not only was he a hero but he was handsome too.

Daphne quickly fell under his spell. He was charming and attentive. Just under six foot tall, slim with dark hair and fine green eyes he was always immaculately dressed and spick and span when wearing casual boating clothes.

Within weeks the couple were together constantly, usually sailing in Tommy's boat. Within eight weeks of their meeting they were planning to marry.

It was on July 19, 1932 that they were married.

It was an unconventional wedding. Daphne wore a blue serge suit and set out on the river with her parents by boat early in the morning to get to the top of Pont Pill which is a tidal creek is opposite the Yacht Club. From the bridge at Pont they walked up the hill to Lanteglos church. Tommy's best man was George Hunkin, his boatman, who had introduced the couple. Together they had sailed up the creek in Tommy's boat and climbed the path to the church to wait for Daphne, no doubt hot from the exertion for the path is steep.

The arrangements were unusual but Daphne had been determined on the plan.

After the wedding in the old church of St Willow at Lanteglos by Fowey, the wedding party returned to Ferryside. From there the couple set off for their honeymoon on *Ygdrasil* sailing to Frenchman's Creek on the Helford River.

★ ★ ★ ★ ★ ★ ★ ★ ★ ★

The du Maurier family had been introduced to Sir Arthur Quiller-Couch and his family by their close family friend James Barrie soon after their arrival in Fowey. Daphne became a regular visitor for Sunday tea at the Haven and a firm friend of Foy Quiller-Couch. She greatly admired Q both for his literary skills but as a person too.

She must have heard descriptions of the funeral convoy of boats carrying the first Commodore, Edward Atkinson, to the churchyard at St Willow at Lanteglos many times. With her sense of theatre the spectacle must have inspired her plans for her own wedding arrangements although one wonders what the others thought of the long uphill climb to the church.

Daphne and Tommy lived the typical unsettled lives of army families but they returned to Fowey whenever they could. Their first child, daughter Tessa, was born in 1933 followed by Flavia in 1937 and Christian, known as Kits, in 1941

When war was declared in 1939, it led to long separations of Tommy from his wife and family.

In 1942 Daphne and the children came back to Fowey to live. They took a rented house at Readymoney Cove which had been the coach house for the mansion on the headland, Point Neptune. It proved to be too small for them and Daphne was restless. Wartime was difficult.

Barbed wire blocked the beach and there was no access to the water. Then came the opportunity to rent the Rashleigh mansion at Menabilly. Just as she had fallen in love at first sight with Fowey so had she done with Menabilly. From her first glimpse of it 20 years before, Daphne had cherished a fantasy of living there. She

The Commodore, 1944-1962, Lt General Sir Frederick Browning.

and her children moved in during the winter of 1943/44. It was bitterly cold.

During the weeks that followed the D Day landings in Normandy 1944 the Allies pushed through France. On September 16, one of the largest airborne attacks of the war was launched in Holland.

Field Marshal Montgomery intended to secure crossings of the rivers Maas, Waal and lower Rhine. The operation was code named 'Market Garden' and well over 5,000 aircraft took part. Three division of paratroops and gliders were dropped deep behind German lines. Lieutenant General Frederick Browning was deputy Commander of the first Allied Airborne Army. He had misgivings about the strategy saying that of the five bridges to be taken the one at Arnhem was a "bridge too far".

However he and his 35,000 troops and equipment were parachuted into German occupied territory. German resistance was greater than expected. The operation was not a success and the troops that survived were eventually evacuated by the allies. By the end of September the operation ended in defeat.

General Browning was safely landed on an airfield in The Midlands and returned for a brief visit to Fowey to see for the first time the home that Daphne had prepared for them at Menabilly. He was surprised by how much she had done.

In December 1944 the club secretary received a letter from General Browning saying that he would accept the office of Commodore. But the affairs of the Royal Fowey Yacht Club must have been far from his mind for in that same month he was appointed Chief in Staff in South East Asia and became Lord Louis Mountbatten's right hand man. Soon he was posted to the other side of the world. There he played a prominent role in the surrender of Japan. He was presented with a sword as part of these ceremonials and later presented it to the Yacht Club. There it was displayed in the reading room.

The war in Europe ended in May 1945. The Commodore, General Browning, wrote from Japan for information as to any contemplated activities of the club and his desire to be of any assistance, but he was too far away to be anything other than titular head of the club. Nevertheless he was re-elected Commodore in his absence in November 1945.

General Browning or Tommy as he was known to his friends returned from the war on July 19, 1946 and was Knighted in the New Years Honours List.

On August 9, 1946, Commodore Lieutenant General Sir Frederick Browning chaired his first meeting at the club. There were several matters on the agenda. It seemed important to restore the life of the club after the interruption to sailing and social recreation that war had imposed.

The committee were keen that there should be a regatta and set a date in August.

Lady Browning and her friend Foy Quiller-Couch had already had preliminary discussions with caterers for the 'at home'. Daphne was keen that the function should be as successful as those in pre war years and wanted to use Q's old guest list. It was a long list as the previous Commodore had invited many guests.

Troy racing was discussed and it was hoped to resuscitate the class and that Troy owners would meet at the club.

It was resolved that air raid shelters and debris should be removed from the car park. This is the only reference to car parking at the club. Even the location of air raid shelters is a mystery. Arrangements were made to renew the billiard table top which had worn out. The committee planned with optimism.

In spite of the enthusiasm for the success of the regatta it made a considerable financial loss. Subscriptions towards it were insufficient to cover costs. Obviously the old custom of inviting guests as Q had done was no longer appropriate. Times had changed and money was short. Also it was suggested that at the next regatta the whole of the club should be thrown open to guests. Confining the party to the billiard room had made for severe congestion.

The Commodore was keen to settle in Fowey. He brought a Troy, number T4, and named it Shimmer. He was keen to buy a boatyard and eager to have a new boat built for himself.

But he was only home for six weeks when he was appointed Military Secretary to the Secretary of State for War. He decided to take a flat in London and to travel to Cornwall to spend weekends with his family but a year later he retired from the army and expected to return to life in Fowey and Menabilly for good.

Tommy was looking forward to more sailing. After the Japanese surrender in 1945 when he was stationed in Singapore he acquired a motor fishing vessel called the *Fanny Rosa*. He had her shipped back to Fowey on a troop ship. She was a large boat with six bunks, ideal for cruising with the family. On her arrival in Fowey she was refitted in Hunkin's Yard. There she was painted a striking blue green which contrasted with her rust coloured sails. Unfortunately Tommy's youngest children, Flavia and Kits, did not enjoy sailing in *Fanny Rosa*. She was very broad in the

"A visit to Cowes." Commodore General Browning brought a motor fishing vessel back from Singapore after the war. He named the boat Fanny Rosa *after a character in "Hungry Hill" a novel written by his wife Daphne du Maurier. In this picture Princess Elizabeth (as she then was) and Prince Philip stand alongside the mizzen mast. General Browning (back view) is standing aft. Holding the mizzen boom is R.T. Bunt in a white cap and also present are Richard Thomas and George Keast, by the wheel house door.*

beam and they were unable to cope with her constant rolling motion. It was the Commodore's eldest daughter, Tessa, who was keen on sailing. She would race whenever she could in the family Troy yacht *Shimmer* in the company of Tommy's boatman, Dick Bunt.

In 1947 Tommy was appointed Comptroller and Treasurer to HRH Princess Elizabeth which meant that we would be in charge of the Princess' household at Clarence House in London. This appointment meant that Tommy, or Boy Browning as he was called by the Royal Household, had to live in London and also accompany Princess Elizabeth and Prince Philip on their trips aboard.

It seemed obvious to Tommy that he could no longer fulfil his rôle as Commodore of the Yacht Club. In July 1947 a letter was read to the Yacht Club committee. The Commodore tendered his resignation. The committee accepted with great regret but asked him to remain in office until the end of the club financial year. However the Commodore was present at a large committee meeting the following month when he announced that he had been asked to continue in office. He explained that it would be very difficult for him to attend meetings often but that he was prepared to continue if the committee accepted this proviso. The meeting unanimously agreed that he should continue as Commodore. They did not want to let him go. During the years that followed most of the management committee meetings where chaired by deputies to the Commodore.

Capt. W. F. Ruffle, Hon. Sec. of the Sailing Committee, philosophically contemplates the calm water of the harbour from the clubhouse railings

YACHTSMEN AT A REGATTA IN CORNISH WATERS

Lack of wind was redressed by good spirits
at the Royal Fowey Yacht Club's event

428   THE TATLER and Bystander SEPTEMBER 14, 1949

Miss Margaret and Mr. Christopher Bulteel talking to Mr. Douglas Marshall, M.P. for Bodmin

Mr. John B. Graham and Dr. R. G. Harcourt watch yachts making the most of occasional puffs

Neat work with a dinghy: Mr. and Mrs. G. D. Luck being rowed ashore by the younger generation after taking part in a race

Lady Howe (foreground), Sir Robert Howe, Governor-General of the Sudan, and Mr. A. T. Holman

The Royal Fowey Yacht Club Regatta is featured in the magazine Tatler and Bystander, September 14 1949.

THE TATLER and Bystander. SEPTEMBER 14, 1949 429

The regatta was directed from the Fanny Rosa, yacht of the Commodore, Lt.-Gen. Sir Frederick Browning. The clubhouse is seen centre background

Miss Ann Crowder, Mr. James Hunter-Blair and Miss Rosemary Crowder watch the racing from Merlin, belonging to Capt. John Crowder, M.P. for Finchley

Mr. J. P. Carter stands by while his son and daughter-in-law, Mr. and Mrs. James Carter, discuss the possibility of a good breeze coming up

Mr. Denys Hodson (behind), nephew of Mr. Justice Hodson, and Mr. Guy Symondson were among the spectators who had a very pleasant afternoon watching the racing

Photographs by David

Mr. J. H. Stokes standing on the deck of his well-found sloop, Lady Prudence, while Miss Tessa Browning, daughter of Sir Frederick and Lady Browning (Daphne du Maurier), and Mr. Stock leave in the dinghy after a sail

HRH The Duke of Edinburgh with Uffa Fox sailing Bluebottle *for International Dragon Class yachts at Cowes.*

The Commodore and The Duke of Edinburgh

In 1952 the Commodore was in Kenya with Princess Elizabeth and the Duke of Edinburgh when the death of King George VI occurred. Princess Elizabeth became Queen and on their return to England Tommy was made Treasurer to the Duke of Edinburgh. He continued in this capacity until his retirement at the age of 62 in 1959, visiting his family at Menabilly whenever be could.

During his time with the royal household, Tommy and the Duke of Edinburgh became friends. On visits to the Browning family at Menabilly the Duke of Edinburgh was able to enjoy sailing from Fowey almost anonymously in the company of his friend.

In May 1952 the Yacht Club had the honour of a visit from Prince Philip one morning. The Commodore introduced him to the club after a visit to the boat yard in Polruan where Prince Philip's Dragon yacht *Bluebottle* was receiving a coat of paint. How remote from life in London it must have seemed. It was in May that year that the Queen and the Duke of Edinburgh took up residence at Buckingham Palace.

At the AGM of the Yacht Club in December 1952 it was resolved to ask Prince Philip to become Patron of the club. By January 12, 1953 HRH The Prince Philip, Duke of Edinburgh had agreed to do so.

1953 was the year of the Coronation. At the meeting the committee discussed the issue of a new rule book. It was to be with gold on the cover, entitled the Coronation Book and to include the history of the Club by Walter Grahame.

On June 8, 1953 the Club management committee met and agreed to send a message of congratulations to the Commodore on his appointment as Knight Commander of the Royal Victorian Order. Also thanks were extended to him for placing his yacht at the disposal of the authorities for the Royal Salute on Coronation Day.

At the AGM in December Tommy was re-elected Commodore in his absence. The Queen and Prince Philip and the Royal household left the UK on 23 November for a six month tour of the Commonwealth accompanied by the Commodore.

Their return from the tour was on the Royal Yacht *Britannia* which had been launched the year before. *Britannia's* first voyage was to Tobruk taking Prince Charles age 5 and Princess Anne to meet their parents after six months separation. They returned on May 15, 1954.

Although the Commodore had been away from Fowey for so long preparations for the Yacht Club regatta were well in hand. It was decided that outside caterers should be employed to provide lunches at 4/6d and afternoon tea at 3/6d. To avoid overcrowding a large awning was to be erected over the terrace and meals served from the flag pole end.

Shortly before the regatta the Commodore sent a message to say that he would be unable to help with the regatta and that he might not be able to sail either. Nevertheless the regatta was a success. It seems that the new arrangements were an improvement as the next two regattas were increasingly popular and successful. At a regatta dance in 1954, 153 tickets were sold and the profit made allowed for a donation of £25 to the RYA's British Olympic Appeals Committee. In fact dances became popular for a while. At first the steward was paid a small token for the loan of his gramophone. Later music for dancing was provided by the club's own radiogram. This acquisition was not approved of by all. A question in the suggestions book asked:

"If it was necessary or desirable to have the gramophone grinding out noises in the morning"

The Commodore's printed reply was "No".

It was with great sadness that he relinquished his rôle in the Royal Household. He officially retired at the age of 62. Everyone hoped that once he was at home with Daphne his health would revive

The Commodore's health began to fail in 1957 but he carried on with his duties at Buckingham Palace until May 1959. At the next management committee of the club the Vice Commodore was able to congratulate the Commodore on the honour conferred on him by Her Majesty on his retirement from the Royal Household namely the Knight Grand Cross of the Royal Victorian Order.

It was in July 1962 that HM The Queen and the Duke of Edinburgh visited the Westcountry. They arrived by Royal train at Saltash and after various visits in the area arrived at Menabilly for tea with Daphne and their old friend Boy Browning.

The day had been Cornwall's hottest day of the year and there have been thundery showers. The Western Morning News reported that the Duke had worn the Royal Fowey Yacht Club tie. The paper also reported that the couple had

"an ordinary family tea. The Duke had been there before but for the Queen it was her first visit and she thought it was a 'lovely old house'. After tea the Royal couple drove into Fowey along a route lined with cheering crowds. At the town quay they embarked for the Royal Yacht Britannia which was moored at the harbour entrance"

Although the Royals did not visit the Yacht Club Tommy was still Commodore and the inevitable choice of club Christmas card that year was a photograph of The Royal Yacht *Britannia* moored at the mouth of Fowey harbour.

Three years later Tommy was forced to offer his resignation from his duties at the club. He had been Commodore for 17 years but he could cope no longer.

At the Annual General Meeting it was decided that Sir Frederick Browning should be made Admiral of the club.

Tommy's health continued to deteriorate. Back in 1943 his left leg had been injured in a glider crash. The damage to his leg gave him great pain and he was no longer able to enjoy sailing. His circulatory problems continued and in January 1965 at St Marys Hospital, Paddington his left foot was amputated. His health did not improve and later in 1965, at the age of 68, he died.

HM The Queen and HRH The Duke of Edinburgh leaving the town quay, Fowey after having taken tea at Menabilly with Daphne du Maurier and Commodore General Browning. The Royal Yacht Britannia *awaits Their Majesties at the harbour mouth, 25 July 1962.*

The new Commodore - Donald Carter

The new Commodore elected in 1962 was Major Donald R Carter. He was a popular choice. Born in Fowey in 1901 he was known and liked by all. When he was 18 he joined the family firm of Toyne and Carter and later became head of the firm.

In 1922 he was Commissioned in Cornwall R E Territorial Army and continued to serve with the Territorials until he was invalided out in 1940. Then for three years he commanded the Fowey, Lanteglos and St Sampson Home Guard unit.

Donald Carter was a member of the lifeboat crew when their service was stationed at Polkerris in the days when it relied on sail and rowing.

He was Secretary of the Fowey branch of the RNLI for 21 years. He was also a member of the Harbour Commission and was made Chairman of that body in 1964 and was Chairman for 10 years

Donald Carter was 19 when he joined the Royal Fowey Yacht Club. He was sailing secretary for many years and was elected Rear Commodore in 1949.

When he became Commodore in 1962, Donald Carter brought his special charm to the club. He is still remembered with affection by many for his hospitable welcome to visitors to the club and for his qualities of dedication. His wife was a keen sailor too.

At the AGM 1974 the retirement of Commodore Donald Carter was announced. He had been in post for twelve years and was now 73. That same year he was elected to Admiral of the club and it was also in that year that Prince Charles agreed to accept Honorary Membership of the Club.

Dr A M Luther was elected to serve as Commodore and did so for 5 years.

Major Donald Carter, Commodore of the Royal Fowey Yacht Club 1962-1974.

The Barclay's Bank Cup

In 1975 the Honorary Treasurer of the club, Mr Bruce Archer, retired from his post at Barclays Bank in the town. Barclays Bank wished to pay tribute to him and also to mark eighty years of the bank's association with the Royal Fowey Yacht Club. It was decided to offer a trophy to the club to be presented for the outstanding nautical achievement of the season by a club member. It is known as the Barclays Bank Cup and is usually presented at the Gentleman's Dinner held on the night of the AGM.

Mr Bruce Archer resigned his post of Honorary Treasurer to the Yacht Club in 1976 after 15 years service.

At the AGM on March 3, 1979 a new Commodore was elected ~ Major O J Lewis. He was to serve in this capacity for three years.

At the dinner which followed the AGM the Barclays Bank Cup was presented to Richard Turpin. He had sailed round the world with his daughter Mary Ann Turpin in his boat *Rumwimata*. Subsequently there was a formal 'welcome home' at the club and a talk when Richard Turpin described the adventure to an audience of club members.

The Barclays Bank cup is not awarded every year. Citations appear sporadically. Lieutenant Commander Jem Tetley won it a second time for winning his section of the Azores race. He was accompanied in his boat *Carte Blanche* by his wife Mor on this trip.

Other winners of the trophy have been M Ellis twice and Harold Eardley.

It was awarded to Rusty Eplett for rescuing a yacht which had run aground at Punches Cross at the harbour mouth during a race.

Mr W Rudgard was awarded the Barclays Bank Cup for his dedication organising safety boats on race days for a number of years. Many will remember him with gratitude including the author of this book who was personally rescued by him and Marcus Lewis.

In 1989 the Barclays Bank Cup was awarded to Nigel Chapman and John Libby. A newspaper report describes their adventure:

"On their return passage of the R.F.Y.C Morgat/Douarnenez Rally, John Libby's yacht *Balladier* sustained underwater damage when in collision with a basking shark. A May Day call was sent out and answered by Nigel Chapman sailing *Sanika* who took *Balladier* in tow. A helicopter later landed a pump to *Balladier* after which *Sanika* resumed the tow for several hours".

The citation recommending the award reads:

"During the whole operation both skippers acted in a calm and seaman like manner which reflected great credit to the club".

One hundred years since the formation of The Fowey Club

During Major O J Lewis' term of office as Commodore it was decided to celebrate one hundred years since the inauguration of the Fowey Club. A committee was formed to organise Centenary celebrations.

On June 25, 1981 a reception was held at the club. There was music from the Police Band and a 'sail past' of boats both sailing boats and motor cruisers and led by a Troy. There were 24 official guests. One hundred and ninety five people attended. Centenary plaques were available at 95p each. The Centenary race prizes were rummers, drinking glasses in 3 sizes.

The celebrations were completed with a Centenary Rally when yachts then sailed to the Royal Western Yacht Club in Plymouth.

The readiness to celebrate and the pattern of festivities has changed very little during the 100 years of the Yacht Club.

During 1982 Mr Piet Mendels formally agreed to make himself responsible for the expense involved in building the new race sailing hut. He was always a generous benefactor. Mrs Eileen Fuller paid for radio sets for the race hut in memory of her husband. There were other bequests, Mr L A Beck presented a dinghy and outboard motor to the club and the Maschinger bequest bought seven three branch candelabra and the block and gavel to be used at meetings and dinners.

At the AGM in 1982 a new Commodore was elected. This time it was Don Rickard who took on the job. The Barclays Bank Cup was presented that year to Lieutenant Commander Jem Tetley for his two handed trans-Atlantic race in his classic Swan *Carte Blanche*.

Another interesting trophy is the Joan Winkle Cup. Joan Winkle and her sister lived at the Winklepicker on Polruan Quay. They sailed a Fowey River boat for many years, never winning. This trophy is presented to sailors for achievement other than winning races. In 1984 it was presented to Marcus Lewis for recovering a Troy boat, T3 named 'Janet', from the West coast of Scotland. He brought the boat back to the port, rebuilt her and now races her rather more successfully than she fared in her early days.

At around this time a private lottery was established within the club by Jimmy Earl. This is now known as the '300' club.

Patterns of administration were slowly changing and like other yacht clubs Commodores and Flag Officers were expected to serve for shorter tenures of office than before.

Major O J Lewis served from 1979 to 1982, D F Rickard from 1982 to 1987 and A G Williams from 1987 until 1992. By contrast during the first sixty four years of the Yacht Club there were only three Commodores.

It was on August 2, 1984 that ex Commodore of the club and Admiral of the club for eight years, Donald Carter died at the age of 83.

Donald Carter was well known and popular in Fowey and there were few associations with which he was not involved. He had joined the British Legion in 1922 and became Chairman of the regional branch and later President. He was Chairman of the old Fowey Rifle Club, Secretary of the Fowey and Polruan branch of the National Trust for 21 years. He was also President of Carlyon Bay Golf Club and Chairman of the old Missions to Seamen's Club and for many years served as Governor to Fowey Grammar School.

When he died it was said "We have lost Mr Fowey himself".

FIT FOR NORTH SEA GALES

Miss Foy Quiller-Couch

Just 2 years later on February 24, 1986, the community lost Q's daughter, "Miss Fowey herself" at the age of 86. Her sailing days were long over but the committee stood for a minute's silence tribute to her. She had served the Yacht Club long and faithfully masterminding the Regatta 'at homes' long before her devotion was officially recognised by special membership.

Foy and Edward Grose working on the farm in later years. Edward Grose was the family boatman. He taught the young Foy to play cricket on the lawn at the Haven.

When her brother Bevil died in 1919 she renounced all plans she might have had for herself and dedicated her life to caring for her parents the Commodore and Lady Quiller-Couch.

She took a keen interest in the events of the town and had many friends including the Rashleighs and Daphne du Maurier. Like her father she was fond of dressing in bright colours. She frequently travelled by boat or by pony and trap. She regularly rode Bevil's horse Peggy. When Q brought Peggy back to Fowey he employed Bill Vincent as groom. Bill and his father had worked with the horses on the jetties loading China Clay and Bill was the inspiration for William Henry in Q's novel 'Castledore'.

In 1975 Foy was awarded the MBE for her work with the National Trust.

She was one of the first honorary lady members of the Yacht Club and proved herself a brave sailor in her boat *Jig Saw* which she had bought in 1923. *Jig Saw* had been built in 1906 by Watty. Until Foy owned her she had been sailed by her father's friend John (Loftus) Long of Fowey.

When Foy left the Haven where she had always lived with her parents she went to live at Trelowarren in West Cornwall. Later she moved back nearer to Fowey and lived at Lanhydrock. There she may have found comfort from her memories of happy associations during her youth. The two families, the Quiller-Couch's and the Agar Robartes, had become good friends during Q's time working for the Liberal Party.

Sixty years of Troy racing

In 1989 a celebration was held at the Yacht Club to mark sixty years of Troy boat racing. On June 17 there was a champagne and buffet reception and racing too. Special prizes were awarded and commemorative plaques were available for purchase.

Mrs Pam Sheridan presented a bronze sculpture to the club. It is of a Troy under sail and was modelled by Mr Tony Lamb and cast in bronze. Mrs Sheridan has sailed and raced the same Troy all her adult life. When she was twenty one she was given a Troy boat by her father Colonel E Treffry. It was number 10 named 'Opal'.

The start of a Troy race from the yacht club terrace, 1950.

Troy class, 1933

Maid of Foye, *the most successful boat in the fleet of Troys being raced
by S.J. Hicks, 1958-63.*

A new Admiral

At the Annual General Meeting in 1990 the membership agreed that Mr Piet Mendels be proposed for the office of Admiral.

Piet Mendels had been elected to the club in 1928, sixty two years previously. He was the oldest friend of the club, and had assisted it in countless ways. He had been Vice Commodore from 1964 to 1968. It was a popular decision that be became Admiral.

His 90th birthday, the next year, was celebrated at the club on April 20, 1991. There was a champagne party on the club terrace and a 'sail past' of boats in his honour.

Vice Commodore Wing Commander Farlow and Mr L.P. Mendels M.B.E. at the inauguration of the sailing and race offices, 10 April 1982. Piet Mendels had funded the project.

Port of Fowey Race Organising Committee (P.O.F.R.O.C.)

In the early 1990's the Port of Fowey Race Organising Committee was established. P.O.F.R.O.C. was constituted from members of the Royal Fowey Yacht Club and the Fowey Gallants Sailing Club in order to share organisation of racing in the harbour on Wednesday, Saturdays and also regatta racing.

The Club hosts the meetings of P.O.F.R.O.C. and also provides the facilities of race officers and computerised results service.

The first Commodore's flagship *Airymouse*

It was in July 1994 that *Airymouse*, the flagship of the first Commodore, Edward Atkinson, came back to Fowey to mark her centenary. She had been launched from Watty's yard in 1894.

Designed for the Commodore by Edwin Brett, her length overall was 58 feet. No expense was spared as Edward Atkinson was a wealthy man. She was two years in the making.

Airymouse is the Cornish name for a bat. The original figurehead was modelled by a Mr Calcott in the shape of a bat with wings folded either side of the prow. The model was cast in gilt bronze at a foundry in London namely Broad and Sons.

A newspaper of the time wrote:

"She was launched on July 12, 1894. As she dipped in the water with a fall of a few feet she shipped a large quantity of water and all on board were swamped. Two pleasure boats got under her stern but fortunately no accident happened. Fowey Town Band under Mr W Hawken played selections. Mr Watty was heartily congratulated on turning out so beautiful a vessel".

Thereafter she sailed with the rich and famous celebrities of the day on board. Edward Atkinson was a sociable and generous host and being wealthy his life was dedicated to pleasure.

When he was drowned in 1911 his cousin Miss Kate Isabel Marston, his executrix, sold *Airymouse*. His Solicitor was a Mr Ernest A Kite of Palace Chambers, Westminster and Miss F Freeman was his typist.

In July 1915 Miss Marston gave the model of the figurehead of *Airymouse* to the club. It was not until August 1951 that Miss Freeman wrote to the Commodore of the Yacht Club offering him the original figureheard of *Airymouse*. It had decorated the Solicitors offices, in which she worked for 40 years, until the firm wound up in 1951.

During the first World War *Airymouse* was shorn of her 3½ ton lead keel and used as a houseboat on the Hamble. Later she was bought by a Mr Bruce Atkey who reconditioned her to a ketch.

Then in June 1925 she was bought by Mr L Boughton Chatwin whose grandson

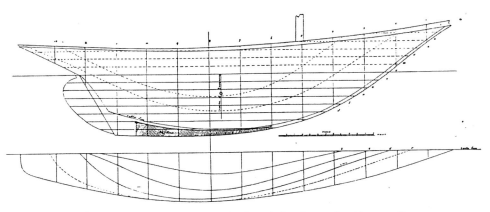

These lines of Airy Mouse reveal a lean, hollow bow and a "long run" at the stern.

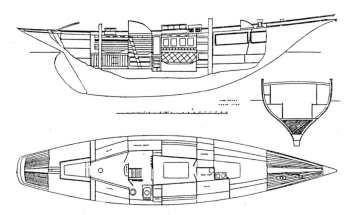

After a 5-tonner, the lay-out seemed palatial.

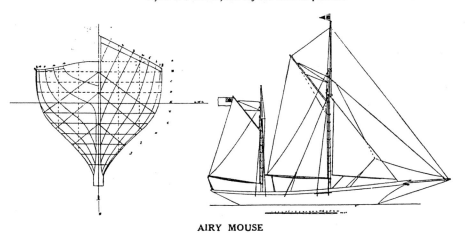

AIRY MOUSE

The body plan is reminiscent of "plank-on-edge" days; but the reduced sail plan, although small, is quite enough for two to handle comfortably in tight corners.

155

"Airymouse" figurehead in bronze.

was Bruce Chatwin. In a collection of his essays entitled 'What am I doing here?', Bruce Chatwin writes:

"In the twenties and thirties, my Grandfather, a Birmingham lawyer, owned a vessel of legendary beauty. She was a teak, clipper-bowed ketch built at Fowey in Cornwall. She had once been rigged as a cutter. An 'airymouse' is a bat and under her bowsprit there was a figurehead of a bat with outstretched wings. The bat had disappeared by my father's day. *Airymouse* had brown sails dyed with cutch bark, a brass ships bell and a gold line from stem to stern.

"My Grandfather died in 1933 and *Airymouse* had to be sold. She needed expensive repairs to her stanchions. Neither my father nor his brothers and sister could afford them. They sold her for £200. For my father alone it was the loss of a lover. He had other boats but he shared them with others and none matched the boat of his dreams.

"I do not think he could bring himself to find out what had happened to *Airymouse*. He heard rumours. In Guernsey a car had driven over the pier and landed on her deck without doing too much damage. Or she was a rotting house-boat in the mud of a West Country creek. Or an incendiary bomb had hit her in the war. He came to accept that she was gone but never quite believed it. On our sailing holidays we all believed that one golden evening off Ushant or in the Race of Alderney two sails would appear on the horizon and the ethereal craft would heave into view. Mr father would raise his binoculars and say the words he yearned to say "It's *Airymouse*".

She had in fact been bought by a marine artist called Torquil McCleod. A car had in fact fallen from the quay in Guernsey onto her deck. Because of her age, Torquil had not been able to afford insurance. It was too expensive for him to have her repaired. Arrangements were made for her to be burnt on the beach but at the eleventh hour, *Airymouse* was reprieved. A young man who had also loved her from a distance since his boyhood rescued her.

By 1960 she was sailing again and then once again lost. There is no account of her until she was rediscovered stripped and rotting in river mud in the 1980's.

This time a young man, Alan Tate, had found her up the River Dart. He too fell in love with her and bought her. He took her to a yard in Totnes. The deck was gone. Many of the oak timbers were gone but the teak hull was in perfect condition. Gradually she was reconstructed and sailed again.

In July 1994 Alan Tate brought her back to Fowey for her centenary. Inside the clubhouse members and guests drank a champagne toast to *Airymouse*. On a mooring off the club terrace, back 'home' again, there she shone teak and white, glowing in the evening sun as beautiful and elegant as she had been in Fowey one hundred years before.

Airymouse, *the cutter built by Watty for the first Commodore, Edward Atkinson. Some time after the figurehead of a bat had been removed.*

The author on board Airymouse *at Mixtow Creek 1994, on the occasion of the centenary visit of the first Commodore's flagship after restoration by Alan Tate.*

Women in the Yacht Club

From the beginning in 1894 when the club began as a Gentleman's Club the company was exclusively male. Women were not admitted to the club except for the 'at home' during Regatta week.

Then in 1902 there was a proposal that members should have the privilege of bringing ladies and children over 12 years of age to the veranda or to the coffee room for tea between the hours of 3pm and 6.30pm. Members were to remain with their guests during the visit.

Three years later it was suggested that permitted hours for lady visitors should be limited from 3pm until 6pm as Dr Morse had complained that the privilege had been used to an unreasonable and annoying degree. There is no record of any response to this curtailment until after the Regatta.

In an account of regatta racing that same year is a record of the first woman helm at Fowey sailing a cutter of four tons. The helmswoman was a Miss Wheeler and her boat was named appropriately *The Saucy Nell*. She was meeting men on their own terms on the water and must have represented something of a challenge.

During the afternoon 'at home' at that Regatta the Royal Artillery Band from Plymouth played for a large mixed gathering of guests. It was noted that the tables were laid out by lady friends and relatives of club members. The catering arrangements for these big gatherings of around 200 guests were always conducted by this regular team of ladies for many years to come. Women who gladly helped the club in this way were not otherwise welcome.

At the next meeting the chairman reminded members 'that having been aquainted with the strong feeling on the subject expressed by Dr Morse and others that the privilege should no longer be used unduly'.

Traditionally women were expected to be subservient to men. They had to know their place which was in the home. Men were considered to be superior to women and entitled to respect from them.

By the turn of the century many women were beginning to question this rôle. The suffragette movement was formed to campaign for political votes for women. The fact that they were not eligible to vote epitomised their discontent. Although the aims of the suffragettes were praiseworthy and reasonable the movement was viewed with disdain by many. From 1903 onwards their actions became increasingly militant involving civil disobedience and much public opinion hardened against them especially amongst those who wanted no change. Suffragette action continued right up to the start of the first World War in 1914. Then it largely ceased as attention turned to supporting war effort. As more and more men left their civilian jobs to fight overseas women stepped in, carrying on men's work.

Within society attitudes to women began to slowly change. There was no such alteration within the Yacht Club. In 1918 the final year of the war the regulations regarding ladies visiting the club were reviewed by the Management Committee. It was agreed that there should be no change and the matter did not come up again for discussion for another twelve years.

The matter might have been closed by the club but in the same year British women over the age of 32 who were householders or the wives of householders or who had been to University were finally granted the right to vote for Members of Parliament. The rest of the female population had to wait another 11 years.

Whatever nationwide debate that was raging regarding the status of women there was little evidence of change within the Commodore's household. Daughter Foy Quiller-Couch was beginning to emerge as a brave helmswomen but this was the only sign of emancipation. Several who remember have described Sir Arthur and Lady Quiller-Couch's Sunday morning ritual. After having attended morning service at St Fimbarrus church where they always sat in the same two seats beside a pillar the couple would make their way to the Yacht Club. Whilst her husband was inside the building having his customary drink with fellow members, Lady Quiller-Couch would sit on a seat on the terrace until it was time to walk back to the Haven together for lunch.

A summer morning on the terrace of the Royal Fowey Yacht Club.

In 1923 when she was 23 years of age Foy Quiller-Couch bought a half decked 16ft boat called *Jigsaw*. It had been commissioned by her father's friend Loftus Long some years before. She began competing regularly in Fowey sailing races. The race was known as the Y race in which a handicap operated for half decked boats of not more that 21ft. The races were usually won by Albert Bunt who sailed a 16ft fixed keel boat called *Maid of Foye*.

The first Troy boat was designed to become a winner in the Y class. Archie Watty a Fowey boat builder designed T1 for Clare Hanson, daughter of Sir Charles Hanson of Fowey Hall. T1 was launched in 1929 and named *Jocelyn*. T2 built soon after was named *Anemone*.

The Troy proved to be a popular design and more boats followed. Colonel Treffry had *Shimmer* built in 1930 to be sailed by his daughter Elizabeth. He gave his other daughter Pamela, now Mrs Sheridan the tenth built Troy boat for her 21st birthday. *Opal* has been in Pam's ownership ever since and has been continuously sailed with famous distinction.

Women were emerging as sailors and obviously gaining the respect of their fathers.

Although the Management Committee were resolute that women could only be admitted to the club on a strictly limited basis there were some club members who were determined to find ways of inviting them in.

In 1925 a member suggested that permission be given to hold occasional dances in the reading room of the club. After all this was the great era of dancing. Up and down the country dances were held regularly in town halls and village halls. This was the age of 'the flappers', bold fun loving women with cropped hair, short skirts and visible silk stockings.

From America came dances that were all the rage, the Charleston, The Black Bottom and the Foxtrot. Jazz was the new dance music. Throughout the land the clergy were scandalised.

When it was suggested that this revolution should invade the Yacht Club the Commodore responded somewhat mildly "that such a radical change in the usages of the club would require further discussion".

The Rear Commodore said he did not think the club was meant for such things and he did not follow the suggestion. The Vicar proposed that such a suggestion should not be entertained. His proposal was carried. However it was by no means a unanimous decision although 16 voted against change, eight members voted for dancing.

At last in 1929 all women over the age of 21 were given the right to vote for Parliament.

★ ★ ★ ★ ★ ★ ★ ★ ★ ★

In the September of 1931 it was proposed that provision should be made for lavatory accommodation for ladies somewhere within the precincts of the club as long as there was no encroachment on any part of existing club premises. The committee authorised £50 for the project. Even so five members voted against this facility being provided.

The lavatory accommodation was finally available in 1932 at a total cost of £58 2s 9d. To the committee's irritation the Steward's wife asked for a rise in salary to clean it. The response was that the Steward was the servant of the club not his wife. The committee was not disposed to increase the Steward's wages.

Further irritation was revealed regarding lady guests. The Honorary Secretary posted a notice saying that lady guests were under no circumstances to be admitted into the clubhouse. This notice was necessary because of the frequent use by ladies of the telephone room. The Honorary Secretary considered under the constitution of the club this was not permissible. His action was endorsed by the committee.

In 1936 a motion was passed at the AGM: "Ladies may be admitted as guests if brought in by a member, subject to such conditions as the committee may from time to time decided." It was decided that ladies could only be brought onto the club front and into the lounge and nowhere else. The Honorary Secretary was instructed to make enquiries about a telephone to be placed in the ladies cloakroom, either a separate slot machine or extension from the clubhouse. This idea was rejected as being costly.

In November 1939 just after the outbreak of World War II a suggestion was made "that ladies be admitted to the Yacht Club as members on a restricted basis in order to give them status. Many remembered how the status of women changed during the first World War.

The committee responded with the following announcement.

"There is no evidence of any general desire that this change in the constitution of the club should be made. No alteration in the rules is advisable".

During the second World War there was no yachting. Many members were away from Fowey in the services and overseas. As in the previous war the Yacht Club had a temporary function as a recreational club for convalescent officers and also for those stationed in Fowey in preparation for war service.

By the end of the war the position of women in society had changed forever. Women had proved themselves equally capable to men.

There were many changes in post-war Britain as society struggled to adapt to the social changes brought about by war and one of the most contentious was the position of women in the community. This was an issue that the Club could not ignore. There was much discussion amongst the membership. Many women related to members were loyal and actively supporting the club but they had no status.

It was not surprising that there was increasing pressure to include women in the club by the membership.

No women members yet.

Although the matter had been raised back in 1944 before the end of the war it was proposed that no alteration be made to the existing rules regarding ladies using the club. Only ladies whose names were in the guest book were allowed to order afternoon tea but they had to notify the steward in advance. Nor were they permitted to buy drinks at the bar.

Women were being constantly relegated by the steward who was acting on the instructions of the management committee.

In any case afternoon teas were plain fare indeed. These post war years were dominated by austerity and rationing persisted. By May 1949 the price of a cup of tea with bread and butter was nine pence. If cakes were provided the price rose to one and sixpence. This simple refreshment was not to everyone's taste and the Hon. Sec was urged to get a permit from the Food Office for cheese and tinned meats so that the sandwiches would be more interesting.

But it was not the quality of the fare that was at issue. It was the fact that although the position of women in society had changed as a result of two world wars nothing had changed in the yacht club in its attitude to women since its formation in the previous century.

In 1949 a sub committee was elected to examine the suggestion of accepting ladies as members of the club.

A questionnaire was circulated in the members and 62.5% of those replied. 69 voted in favour of accepting lady members whilst 57 were in favour of continuing to exclude women. Nine members wrote back to say that they were still doubtful. Their indecision reflected the indecision of the committee. There was discussion but the matter was deferred until the Commodore and Vice Commodore could be present. Perhaps they could rescue the committee from this paralysis of indecision.

Six months later there was a sign of change when it was suggested that ladies who are wives or daughters, over 18, of members could be invited to join the club as family members.

During the summer there was a further proposal this time that there should be some sort of provision in the club for ladies, not just toilets. These were times of extreme post war austerity. Nevertheless it was agreed that the billiard table should be sold and the room converted into a common room for the use of ladies as well as men. The estimated cost for refurbishment was £200. Subsequently the billiard table and balls were sold for £50. There was a great deal of discussion about these radical proposals and a decision was reached that there should be a separate entrance for ladies at the South end of the property!

The constitutional amendments proposed were worked out in detail.

The radical change anticipated was that members should be entitled to nominate wives and daughters over 18 as family members.

Special membership was envisaged on a yearly basis to a number of ladies who were known to be exceptionally distinguished for their sailing activities. There were to be no more than 12 special members.

It was suggested that men members, family members and special members should be entitled to introduce temporary lady members for a period of not more that four weeks in a club year.

Subscription rates should be £2.2s for the first family in port member and £1.16s for others and out port family members £1.1s and 10s 6d respectively.

These changes were all adopted at the next AGM by a majority vote. It is interesting that there were 97 members present voting for the changes whilst 38 members voted against family membership.

Progress was slow regarding the structural adaptations. Licence to proceed was refused by the Ministry of Works in Bristol as it was not considered to be a matter of urgency. The estimated cost rose to £450 and at the AGM in 1951 there was concern about pressing on with the project.

Nevertheless the committee voted to continue and it was decided to fund the work with an issue of £25 debentures. These were quickly taken up. In fact the project was over prescribed.

It was in 1967 that Rear Commodore Maxwell Hyslop put forward the thought that soon we should consider making a special class of lady members since ladies now participate in so many things on equal terms with men.

Questioned as to whether he intended them to enter fully into club life, sit on committees, vote or even hold office he replies that he had not considered these points.

It was decided to record the discussion so that if and when the time came about it would be appreciated that the ideas had been mooted in 1967.

The question of full membership for ladies recurred during tenures of succeeding Commodores.

Prior to the AGM in 1984 a paper was circulated to the membership setting out the options. At the meeting when 92 members were present. 69 of them wished to maintain the rules. 27 voted to admit ladies to full membership.

Again in 1991 it was agreed to maintain the status quo and not allow full membership for women.

By October 1994 the tide of opinion within the club had largely changed and matched attitudes to women in society at large. Ladies at last became eligible for full membership of the club. During the Spring, a questionnaire had been sent to members inviting them to indicate their preference. There were 63 replies of which 45 were in favour of lady membership. A ballot at the AGM in 1994 resulted in 70 members voting for the proposal. The feeling was not unanimous. 17 voted against admitting women as full members of the club. Women now have full voting rights, sit on committees and are entitled to hold office, a vindication of the entry in the Suggestions Book in 1967 by Rear Commodore Maxwell Hyslop.

Since the decision by the membership in 1994 to admit women to the club as members in their own right with full voting powers there have been four women elected to the management committee ~ Jill Selbie, Penny Jones, Chris Thomas and Sylvia Anson. Jill and Penny have both served full terms of three years and at the AGM 2000, two more women have been elected to management ~ Jennifer McKone and Janet Howard.

Honorary membership for Pete Goss

Honorary membership of the Royal Fowey Yacht Club for Pete Goss, April 1998. Left to right: G. Coombs, Rear Commodore, T. King, Rear Commodore, Pete Goss, Denis Simpson, Commodore, M. Mitchell, Sailing Secretary, J. Libby, Vice Commodore.

In April 1998 The Royal Fowey Yacht Club was honoured by a visit from Pete Goss. So many wanted to hear his account of the terrifying rescue that the club accommodation was insufficient to house the audience. The event took place at Fowey Community School. When Pete Goss' modesty and charm endeared him to everyone.

Afterward there was a reception at the club. Pete Goss was invited to accept honorary membership of the club and was presented with an engraved decanter as a token of the admiration in which he is held.

It was in March 1997 that British solo yachtsman Peter Goss sailed into the Biscay port of Les Sables d 'Olonne as a hero. He was cheered by 100,000 admirers who lined the harbour when he arrived at the end of the Vendee Globe single handed race after having rescued a fellow competitor Frenchman Raphael Dinelli.

The start of the Vendee Globe challenge was on November 5, 1996 when Pete Goss sailed south in his 50foot boat *Aqua Quorum*. It was just before Christmas one and a half months later when the barometer dropped 46mB in 24 hours. The wind went from 20 to 60 knots. A large and vicious sea set in made worse by a cross swell. *Aqua Quorum* had already suffered knockdown twice with terrifyingly steep waves threatening to pitch pole the boat.

Then the message came from the race organisers asking him to turn back and sail 160 miles into the teeth of the 60 knot storm to help Raphael Dinelli. *Algimouss* had pitch poled and sunk leaving Raphael Dinelli alone in his life raft west of Australia. For 36 hours *Aqua Quorum* beat into appalling conditions and was repeatedly knocked down. Pete Goss confessed that he came close to his own limits.

With the help of the Royal Australian Air Force Pete Goss located Raphael Dinelli and pulled him from the life raft. He was suffering from hypothermia, weak and ill and required 'intensive care' from Pete Goss during the following days of rest and recovery. Pete Goss had turned South once again into the race route and was able to drop Raphael Dinelli off at Hobart in Tasmania and thence carry on with the race.

By the time he reached the finishing port in France he had been sailing for over four months.

At the finish Pete Goss was awarded the Legion d'Honneur by the French for his outstanding bravery.

One hundred years in the new Yacht Club building

On August 7, 1998 there were celebration to mark one hundred years since the opening of the new club house of the Yacht Club. A special service at St Fimbarrus Church was followed by an afternoon regatta which followed as closely as possible the sailing programme of a century ago. A champagne reception followed whilst the Lostwithiel Town Silver Band entertained. Members and guests, many of whom were dressed in period costume, drank a toast to the future of the club.

One hundred years is a long time. Change is inevitable.

Perhaps the membership have been wary of change for fear of losing something rare at the Royal Fowey Yacht Club. In 1995 as a result of Jimmy Winscombe's legacy the club was re-roofed but nothing changed in the appearance of the club. Members of one hundred years ago would recognise it as being the same building that they had worked so hard to establish. Apart from the bricks and mortar something else lingers here that is rare and valuable. It has something to do with the life and times of a century ago, a microcosm, an atmosphere of courtesy and charm and old protocols, a living memory of what it must have been like to be alive then.

Cynthia - first in Channel Race from Falmouth.

FOWEY BASH

Fizz 'n' Glitz

T HE gods were smiling last month when the prestigious Royal Fowey Yacht Club held its centenary celebration on the sunniest weekend seen yet this summer. The glittering 100th anniversary celebrations which were held over two days of glorious sunshine, included a Champagne reception, Victorian costume, jazz on the terrace, and a special centenary regatta.

Clockwise from top right: Jackie Mitchell and Rosie Smith; Harry and Ann Mainwaring; the Royal Fowey Yacht Club; Rear Commodore Tony King and wife Molly; John Smith, Commodore Denis Simpson and Capt. Mike Mitchell.

FOWEY BASH

Rear Commodore Gordon Coombs and wife Dr Joan Coombs and Monica and Stanley Bourne.

John and Jenny Killingbeck, Dr Martin Luther and Mary Popham.

David and Mary Skerrett, Tessa and Gerry Williams and Major John Lewis with wife Honor

John Nuttall-Smith, Jane Hill and Sue Nuttall-Smith

Catherine and David Burdekin and Karl Stansfield.

George Cussans and Susie and Al Trenary

Twinkle Carter

Peter Geare

Celebration to mark 100 years in the new yacht club building, 1898 to 1998.

In Conclusion

One hundred years ago in 1898 there were 134 members of the Yacht Club, now in 2000 there are 778. In the words of Walter H Grahame the first historian of the club "From that day in 1898 the club had flourished exceedingly thanks in large measure to the guidance and enthusiasm of its Commodores, first Edward Atkinson, then Sir Arthur Quiller-Couch, followed by Lieutenant General Sir Frederick Browning". Walter Grahame was writing in the new book of rules issued to commemorate the Coronation of Her Majesty Queen Elizabeth in 1953.

Since that date there have been nine Commodores. The life of the club continues to flourish and though times change the love of sailing does not.

Denis Simpson, the previous Commodore, writes:
"As Commodore my life revolves around the Club year. For me this starts and ends at each Annual General Meeting. This marks the start of the sailing year. Members are discussing anti fouling and when their craft will be on the water again. Then as if by magic the harbour comes to life and the yachts are on their moorings.

Regular visitors mark the summer months. The HMS Raleigh visit is always in June followed by visits from other clubs along the coast, the Royal Western Y C, the Royal Cornwall Y C and Mylor Y C 'Epic ventures' stop over during their round Britain rally and there is an annual visit of 'Sailing for the blind'.

There is no doubt that the highlight of the year is Regatta Week. Since the beginning it has been a popular venue for sailors up and down the coast".

Toby West, that famous skipper of the Falmouth Working Boat *Victory* arrives accompanied by a flotilla of working boats and their crews from Falmouth. Toby recalls "apart from the war years I don't think I've missed sailing to Fowey Regatta a dozen years". He also recalls "My father and three sons were racing against each other in the Sunbeam class, Falmouth to Fowey, two races up there and a race back to Falmouth", this just after the war.

For summer cruising visitors The Royal Fowey Yacht Club provides a welcome port of call. R Makowski from France writes in the suggestions book in 1964 "I found this club a very friendly place. I'll ever remember as one of the best memories of my holiday. I thank you for this".

As Walter Grahame wrote in his history of the club:
"The Royal Fowey Yacht Club is widely known as a friendly and hospitable place. It's clubhouse is pleasantly set on surely one of the most picturesque waterfronts in the Kingdom. The harbour itself is one of the beauty spots of the West Country and safe in all weathers for all manner of yachts.

"Members of the Yacht Club may be grateful for their heritage and proud to sail under the red burgee bearing the Arms of the Duchy of Cornwall surmounted by the Crown of the eldest son of the Sovereign".

Many share the experience of the young Arthur Quiller-Couch who after seeing Fowey harbour for the first time found that it was 'love at first sight'. Fowey has not changed much and nor have the pleasures to be found here.

In a "Fowey Garland" Q wrote:

> Oh the harbour of Fowey
> Is a beautiful spot,
> And its there I enjowey
> To sail in a yot;
> Or to race in a Yacht
> Round a mark or a buoy
> Such a beautiful spacht
> Is the harbour of Fuoy! . . . . . .

The Royal Fowey Yacht Club

Patron

H.R.H. The Prince Philip, Duke of Edinburgh, K.G., K.T., O.M., G.B.E.

Past Admirals

1963-1965	Lt. General Sir Frederick Browning, G.C.V.O., K.B.E., C.B., D.S.O., D.L.
1976-1984	Major D.R. Carter, T.D.
1990-1996	L.P. Mendels, M.B.E.

Past Commodores

1894-1911	Edward Atkinson
1911-1944	Sir Arthur Quiller-Couch
1944-1962	Lt. General Sir Frederick Browning, G.C.V.O., K.B.E., C.B., D.S.O., D.L.
1962-1974	Major D.R. Carter, T.D.
1974-1979	Dr. A.M. Luther
1979-1982	Major O.J. Lewis
1982-1987	D.F. Rickard
1987-1992	A.G. Williams
1992-1994	L.H. Roberson
1994-1997	Capt. J.G. Wilson, D.S.C., R.D., R.N.R.
1997-2000	D.A. Simpson

Present Commodore

2000-	G.R. Coombs

Edward Atkinson
1893 - 1911

Sir Arthur Quiller-Couch
1911 - 1944

Lt General Sir Frederick Browning
Admiral, 1963 - 1965

Major Donald Carter
1962 - 1974
Admiral, 1976 - 1984

Dr. A.M. Luther
1974 - 1979

Major O.J. Lewis
1979 - 1982

D.F. Rickard
1982 - 1987

A.G. Williams
1987 - 1992

L.H. Roberson
1992 - 1994

Capt. J.G. Wilson
1994 - 1997

Denis Simpson
1997 - 2000

G.R. Coombs
2000 -

Selected Bibliography

Brittain M A, F: *Arthur Quiller-Couch ~ A Biographical Study of Q*,
Cambridge University Press, 1947
Chalmers: *Letters to Austin Purves 1908-15*
Chatwin, Bruce: *What am I doing here*, Picador
du Maurier, Daphne: *Vanishing Cornwall*, Penguin Books
du Maurier, Daphne: *Enchanted Cornwall*, Michael Joseph Ltd
du Maurier, Daphne: *Myself When Young ~ The Shaping of a Writer*,
    Arrow Books 1993
Forster, Margaret: *Daphne du Maurier*, Chatto and Windus, London
Dunbar, Janet: *J M Barrie ~ The Man Behind the Image*, Collins
Graham, Michael: *The Troys Boats of Fowey*, Windjammer Publishing
Grahame, Kenneth: *The Wind in the Willows*, Methuen Children's Books Ltd
Green, Peter: *Beyond the Wild Wood ~ The World of Kenneth Grahame*,
    Grange Books
Irving, John: *The Kings Britannia*, London Seeley Service and Co Ltd,
    196 Shaftesbury Avenue, The Lonsdale Library 1937
Keast, John: *The Book of Fowey*, Barracuda Books Ltd
Leng, Flavia: *Daphne du Maurier ~ A Daughters Memoirs*,
    Mainstream Publishing Company (Edinburgh) Ltd
Mead, C J H: *The History of the Royal Cornwall Yacht Club 1871-1949*,
    Underhill (Plymouth) Ltd
Pickering, Isabel: *Some Goings On*, Published by Isabel Pickering
Prince, Alison: *Kenneth Grahame ~ An Innocent in the Wild Wood*,
    Allison and Busby
Rowse, A L: *A Cornish Childhood*, The Cornish Library
Rowse, A L: *Quiller-Couch ~ A Portrait of Q*, Methuen, London
Quiller-Couch, Sir Arthur: *The Astonishing History of Troy Town*,
    Anthony Mott Limited, 1983
Wesley, Hetty: *Sir Arthur Quiller-Couch*, J M Dent and Sons
Quiller-Couch, Sir Arthur: *Hocken and Hunken ~ A Tale of Troy*,
    J M Dent and Sons Ltd
Quiller-Couch, A T: *From a Cornish Window*, J W Arrowsmith,
    Cambridge University Press
Quiller-Couch, Arthur 'Q': *Memories and Opinions ~ An Unfinished Autobiography*,
    Cambridge Press 1945
Shaw, T W B: *Chronicles of the Royal Western Yacht Club of England 1900-1977*,
    Suttons (Paignton) Ltd

Ward-Jackson, C H: *Ships and Shipbuilders of a Westcountry Seaport Fowey 1786-1939*, Twelveheads Press

West, Arthur: *A Sailing West ~ The Autobiography of Arthur 'Toby' West*, Wordfactory, Falmouth

Yachting Monthly. No.311. March 1932. September 1911.

Illustration Credits

The publishers wish to thank the following for supplying illustrations

Twinkle Treffry: 28, 29, 115, 156.
The National Maritime Museum, Greenwich: 14, 20, 21, 22, 25, 46, 51, 55(upper).
Marcus Lewis and Sue. Rodwell: 73.
The President and Fellows of Trinity College, Oxford: 84, 95, 96, 102.
Guy Symondson: 52, 65, 67, 106, 149.
The late Tony Parkin: 75, 82, 83, 99(upper).
Christine Alexander: 31.
Anthony Buckley & Constantine Ltd.:8.
Beinecke Library, Yale University: 63.
David Turpin: 109.
Jim Matthews and Billie Graeme:16, 37, 40, 54, 55(lower), 72, 63(lower), 95, 175.
The Tatler Magazine: 139, 140.
Mrs. Mavis Johns: 137.
Yachting Monthly Magazine: 17, 18, 33, 62, 75, 78, 93, 111, 117, 148, 168.
Alison Prince: 64.
Mr.and Mrs. Don Lowe :39.
Flavia, Lady Leng:135.
Dr.A.M.Luther:176.
Major O.J.Lewis:176.
Tessa and Gerry Williams:19, 59, 160.
Don Rickard:176.
Denis Simpson:177.
Capt. John Wilson:177.
Cornwall Today Magazine:169, 170.
Royal Fowey Yacht Club:30, 38, 42, 43, 47, 48, 49, 57, 71, 76, 112, 114, 118, 119, 120, 123, 124, 125, 126, 141, 144, 145, 150, 151, 152, 153, 155, 163, 166, 175.

Index